Blue Cypress has magic...
The lake is large.
Even in a canoe it does not take long
to be by ourselves in the surrounding beauty.
It can restore my sense of balance,
feeling of peace...
How good it is
to put aside the burdens of home and work.

Photographs, History and Poems of
the Headwater Lake of the St. Johns River

by

Richard H. Baker, Ph.D. & Juanita N. Baker, Ph.D.

All proceeds from this book will be donated to the Pelican Island Audubon Society.
All photographs were taken from a canoe at Blue Cypress Lake.

ISBN 0-9746115-0-6

Printed by Abbott Printing Co. of Maitland, Florida

Published by the Pelican Island Audubon Society
P.O. Box 1833
Vero Beach, FL 32961
772-567-3520
piaudubon@earthlink.net
www.pelicanislandaudubon.org

Dedication

To Brenda Baker,
with love,
who has shared many
experiences in nature
with us including
Blue Cypress Lake,
helped us with
the artistic layout and encouraged
us
to complete this project.

And

To Gayle and Fergie Peters who
have taken steps to help preserve
the natural beauty of our world
and generously
supported our efforts.

We are deeply grateful to:

Paul Gray, Ph.D. (Audubon of Florida)
Barbara Beidler Kendrick (Belmont, CA)
B.T. Cooksey, Cindy Davis, & Kevin Doty (Blue Cypress Villagers)
Peter Holman (Blue Cypress Ranch)
Brenda Baker, Ph.D.,M.D. & Andy Liu, Ph.D. (Boston, MA)
Marvin Carter (Carter & Associates)
David Dickel, Ph.D. (Department of State, State of Florida)
Clarence F. Korker (Fellsmere, FL)
Rodney Tillman (Fellsmere Water Control District)
Gordon Patterson, Ph.D. (Florida Institue of Technology)
Janice Broda, Phil Lounibos, Ph.D. & Jim Newman
(Florida Medical Entomology Laboratory, IFAS, University of Florida)
Scott Mitchell (Florida Museum of Natural History, Gainesville, FL)
Olske Forbes (Ironside Press)
Patricia Jones (Indian River County Clerk to the Board)
Ruth Stanbridge (Indian River County Historian)
Pat Brown (Indian River County Property Appraiser Office)
Pamela J. Cooper (Indian River County Main Library)
Linda Lovett (Lovett Productions)
Bob Gross, Joy Patterson, & Edward Vosatka (Melbourne, FL)
Jeanne & Joe Middleton (Middleton Fish Camp)
Nancy Prentice (Naples, FL)
Jim Neal, IV (Newark, DE)
Maggy Bowman, Joe Carroll, David Cox, Ph.D., Lynne Larkin, Nancy Irvin, Tina Marchese,
Pat Sawyer, Bob Smith, Barbara Tilney, & Ellie Van Os (Pelican Island Audubon Society)
Paul Tritaik (Pelican Island Wildlife Refuge)
Earl Cason (Port St. Lucie, FL)
Robert Wells (Sebastian, FL)
Mary Ann Lee, Ph.D., Steve Miller, Marc Minno, Ph.D. Matthew O'Malley, Judith H.
Salyers, & Ken Synder (St. Johns River Water Management District)
Judy Orcutt, John Orcutt, Gayle Peters & Ferguson Peters (Vero Beach, FL)
David Baggerley, George Maloney, & Pat Woolwine (Winn Dixie Stores)

CONTENTS

POEMS

FORWARD

America is a rich land, and it is our responsibility to bequeath at least a remnant of that richness to future generations. We must retain wild places where nature can function in all its complexity, variety, and harmony. We need places where birds can fly without fear, fish swim in freedom, and humans discover inner peace and the sound of silence. We are all responsible, everyone, for protecting the small natural treasures in our communities, and we must treat them with both respect and compassion.

Richard and Juanita Baker are shining examples of passionate advocates for one such site, Blue Cypress Lake. They speak on behalf of the ospreys, alligators, and dragonflies, and for the secret places in this wilderness. In this book they are fighting for the lake, striving with clarity of purpose and eloquence to protect its beauty and awaken the conscience of the community to its intrinsic value. May many others join them in this mission.

George B. Schaller
Wildlife Conservation Society

Introduction

Blue Cypress Lake is one of the few undisturbed places in Indian River County, Florida, still natural, and not destroyed by development. Although decades ago some magnificent trees were felled, since then the plants and animals have generally been left untouched, and the lake little affected by human influences. Why has Blue Cypress Lake been spared? Most other lakes in Florida have not only been developed but also compromised by the discharge of nutrients and other pollutants from human activities, the siltation from forest clearing, and the infiltration of exotic plant species such as water hyacinth and hydrilla that clog water bodies and change the lakes' chemical composition. We think it is important for the future of this and other pristine lakes to share with you our story—what we have experienced and learned about this unusual place.

A "headwater" is defined as the source from which a river rises. It is a beginning point. It is also the origin of what is to come. By returning to the source we gain insight into where we came from and who we are. The reward for going to the source is grounding, realizing what is most important and answering questions about who we are. We can go to Blue Cypress as the headwater lake of the mighty St. Johns River, Florida's longest river, flowing over 300 miles north through Jacksonville and east to the Atlantic Ocean, draining about one-sixth of Florida. Blue Cypress Lake reflects not only the sky and the air we breathe but also the area's unique history, which leads us to the source of understanding of how it came to be the way it is today. We bring attention to what is happening both to humans and our wilderness in this little corner of the world. Having fallen in love with Blue Cypress Lake, we write and reflect in several different voices. The descriptions and stories give a vivid and factual account of the lake's journey since its very beginnings. We hope our poems and photographs provide a reflective and artistic perspective of the lake today. We want these different perspectives to take you on a voyage to a greater appreciation of Blue Cypress Lake, one of Florida's natural treasures.

Since 1990, we have visited Blue Cypress Lake many times, often spending the night listening to a steady chorus of frogs and an occasional alligator. It has been a retreat and a solace. Rising before the sun, we get out on the lake to witness the rapidly changing light, and to photograph and savor each moment. The images recorded are one of a kind, never to be repeated. The sun, clouds, and atmosphere will never be exactly that way again. We often see trunks, stumps, roots, and driftwood from trees no longer living, as sculptures, or "found art." Yet wood deteriorates, eaten by insects, impacted by weather, worn away by water, and pecked at by birds in search of food, altering these sculptures again with every peck. Each photograph, therefore, preserves a unique experience. There is magic in these moments. Spending time in nature creates a curiosity to know such a special place better, a desire to capture its feel and to marvel, and then an enthusiasm to share it with everyone. Yet we hesitate, because we want those who visit to continue to respect and preserve it.

Every time we visit, we see something new, something we had missed or that was not there before. The more we learn about a place, the more we come to love and appreciate it. Much of it is only visible to people who can gain access via boats, diving gear, or by slogging through swampland. Birds probably have the easiest access to the area, but we have found that a canoe drawing only six inches allows us into areas where larger motorboats cannot venture.

Learning fascinating stories raises questions we share with you. Why was the lake lost? Why was the lake named what it was? Why is this lake preserved? What prehistoric animals roamed here? What's behind the name Moonshine Bay? How did "Jackass Junction" become more politically correct? Who were the characters living at Blue Cypress Lake a century ago? Through photographs, stories, and poems, we attempt to reflect the essence of Blue Cypress and give credit and appreciation to those who have bequeathed to us Blue Cypress Lake in nearly pristine condition.

NATURAL WONDERS: PRESENT-DAY BLUE CYPRESS LAKE

THE BIG PICTURE

Blue Cypress Lake is approximately 30 miles west of Vero Beach, Florida, north of State Road 60, and seven miles east of the Florida Turnpike at Yeehaw Junction. Turning off SR 60 toward the lake onto a five-mile bumpy, dusty, and washboard road, we frequently see deer, alligators, otters, and wild hogs, and many species of birds including wild turkeys, sandhill cranes, herons, and, when birdhouses are present, numerous Eastern bluebirds. Blue Cypress Village resident and Vero Beach Attorney Kevin Doty has personally observed Florida panther tracks on Blue Cypress Lake road several times since the year 2000 (personal communication, December 9, 2001). His observation is supported by the internet tracking maps provided by the Florida Fish and Wildlife Conservation Commission that show Florida panther #62 traveling on the west side of Blue Cypress Lake.[35] Deer kills by panthers were found in the Fort Drum area in the mid-1990s.

Florida is blessed with more than 7,800 lakes over an acre in size. Its nearest parallels are in Canada and the formerly glaciated northern states from Minnesota to Maine.[8] At 10.2 square miles,[70] Blue Cypress Lake is Florida's twentieth largest natural lake and the largest natural freshwater lake in Indian River County. It measures roughly 4.8 miles long and 3 miles wide.

From its beginning in the lake at 23 feet above sea level, the St. Johns River flows north 310 miles and spills into the Atlantic Ocean east of Jacksonville Florida. During the final 100 miles of its journey, the river's average width is two miles. In 1997, President Bill Clinton designated the St. Johns River an "American Heritage River." The Timucuan Indians first called it Welaka, meaning "chain of lakes."[68] Later, the early French Huguenots called the river May and built Fort Caroline at its mouth. The Spanish captured the fort on September 20, 1565.[59] When Florida was ceded to the United States in 1821, the river was called the San Juan, named after a mission at its mouth, the San Juan del Puerto. The "River of Lakes," as author William Belleville[3] refers to it, is divided into Upper, Middle, and Lower Basins. Blue Cypress Lake is the first link in the chain of six lakes (including Hell'n Blazes, Sawgrass, Washington, Winder, and Poinsett, respectively) that defines the Upper Basin. They encompass a large floodplain (Figure 1). The Atlantic Coastal Ridge (sometimes referred to as the Ten Mile Ridge) bounds it on the east (a natural drainage divide between the St. Johns River Basin and the Indian River Lagoon Basin) and the Kissimmee River Basin on the west.[58] The eastern edge of Blue Cypress Lake is surrounded by flooded marsh and the western edge by hardwood swamp forest.

Before human development, Blue Cypress Lake was surrounded on its north, east, and south by the second largest freshwater marsh in Florida. The largest is the Everglades. The lake gets its water principally from rain and the drainage from the southeast through Mudfish Slough (water flowing intermittently from Fort Drum Swamp or Creek), southwest through Padgett Branch (creek), and west from small creeks, the largest being Blue Cypress Creek, as well as from the water seeping and filtering from the surrounding wetlands (Figures 2 and 3).

Before the lake was mapped, the early 1856/1859 military maps of the area show major drainage leading into the southward extension or opposite direction of the flow of the St. Johns River, which seems, in part, to correspond to Fort Drum Creek, Padgett Branch, and Blue Cypress Creek. John Fries, who first mapped the lake in 1895, describes in an undated letter (housed at the Florida State Library, in Talahassee) the vast marsh surrounding the lake as having three outlets when the waters were in high flood: the St. Johns River, St. Sebastian River and St. Lucie River. However, during normal water levels, only the St. John's River showed a very sluggish flow from the marsh, although there was no distinct channel. Joe Carroll, a local naturalist who was formerly with the U. S. Fish & Wildlife Service indicates that as late as the 1960s, water south of State Road 60 in the Fort Drum area, especially after a heavy rain, could go either north or south, perhaps via Taylor Creek, which empties into Indian River Lagoon at Fort Pierce (personal communication, August 2003). Presently, the large M canal, first dug in 1913, drains the north end of the lake, allowing water to flow north towards Lake Hell'n Blazes (Figure 3).

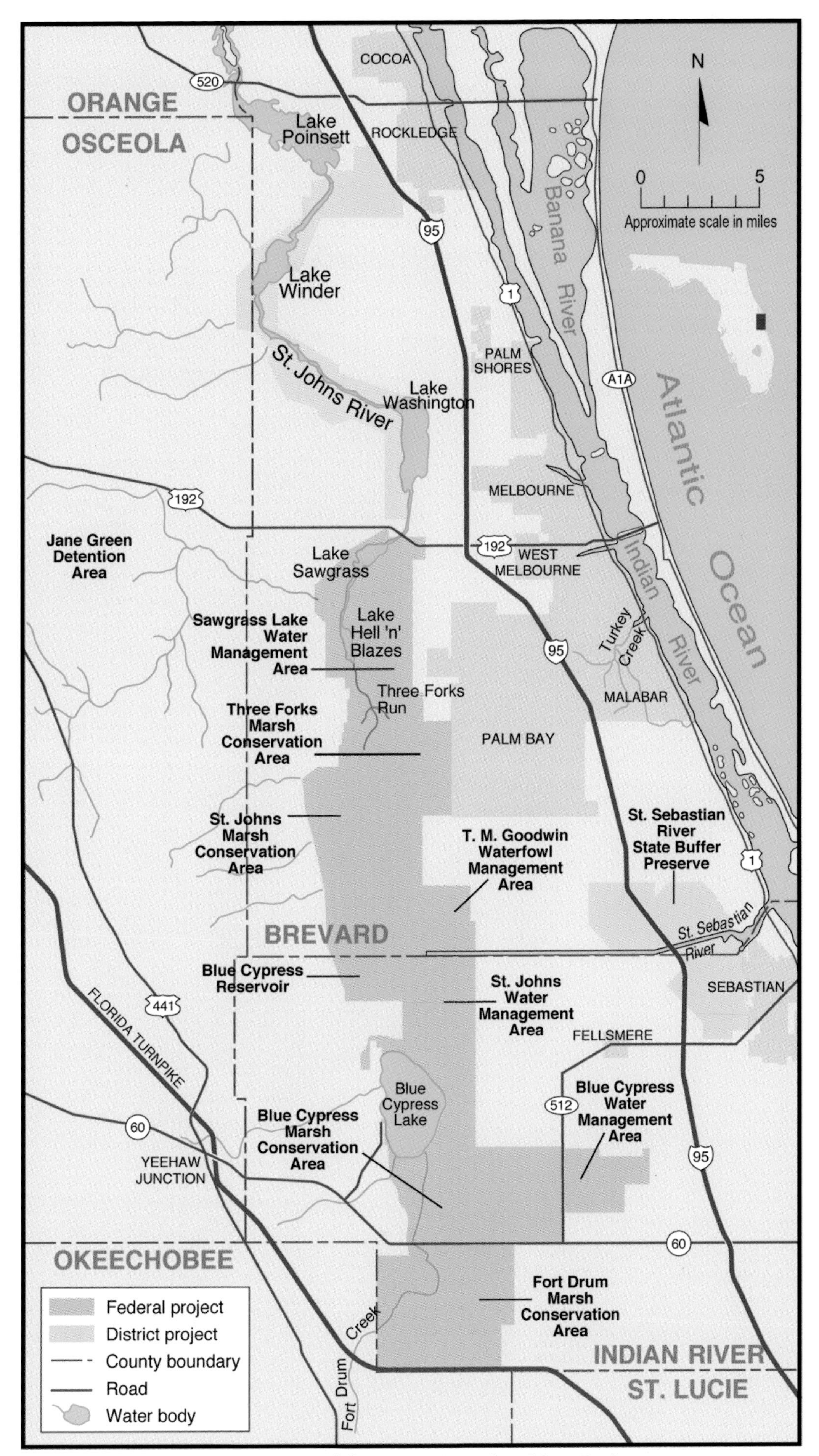

Figure 1. Map of the Upper St. Johns River Basin

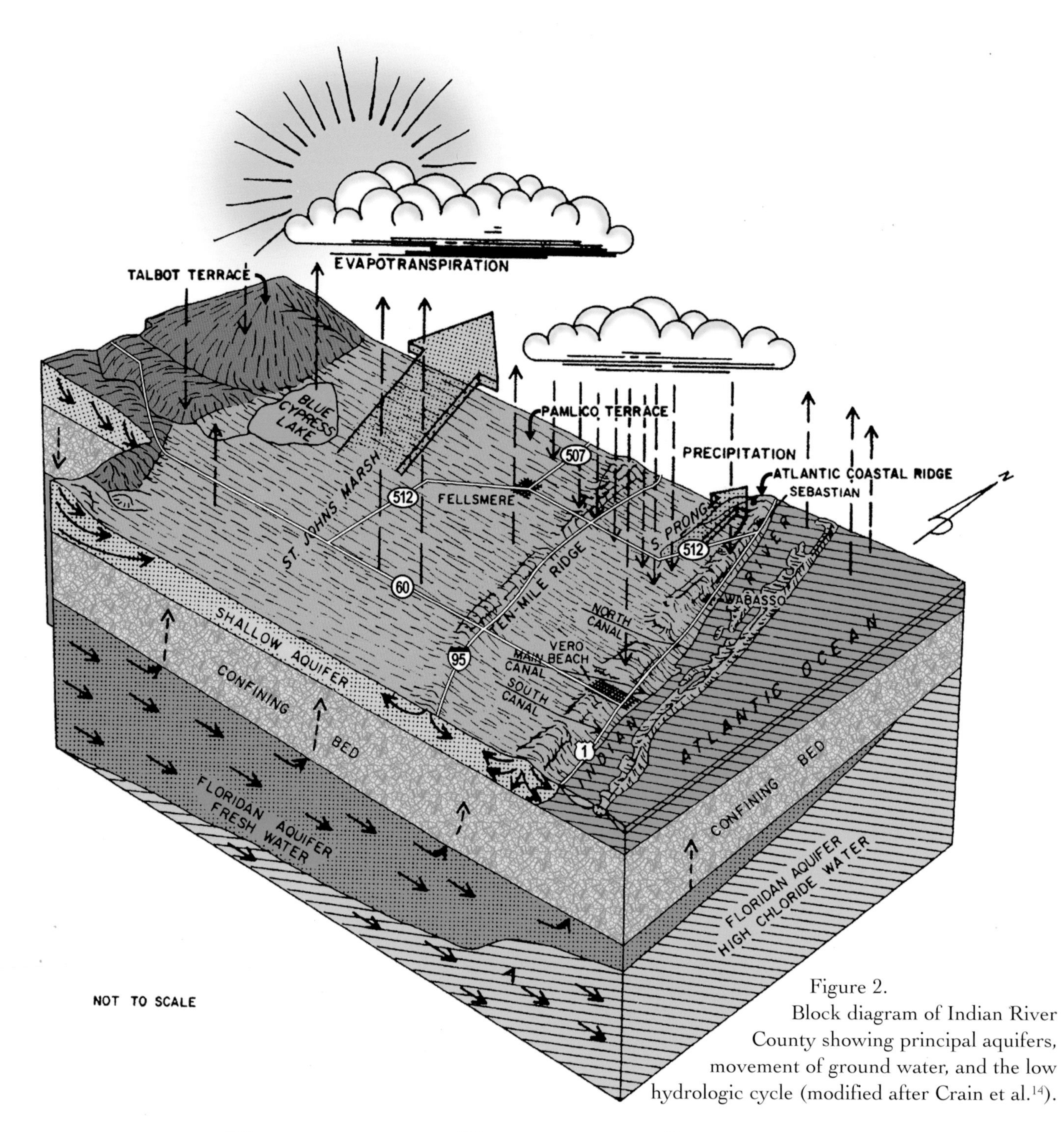

Figure 2.
Block diagram of Indian River County showing principal aquifers, movement of ground water, and the low hydrologic cycle (modified after Crain et al.[14]).

Healthy and Dangerous Lake

Distinguished by its pristine beauty, good water quality and highly regarded fishing for largemouth bass and black crappie (known locally as 'specs')," Blue Cypress is classified as being a mesotrophic lake ecosystem.[105] "Mesotrophic" means that it is intermediate between eutrophic, or "well nourished" with high concentrations of nitrogen and phosphorus, and oligotrophic or "poorly nourished" with low concentrations of nitrogen and phosphorus.[8] Compared to the other marshes and lakes in the basin, Blue Cypress Marsh, which surrounds the lake, is an extensive natural marsh, minimally impacted by human activities. This marsh is essential to preserving the food sources for wildlife and the quality of water flowing into and around the lake system.[64]

The average depth of Blue Cypress Lake is 7.8 feet with the deepest levels reaching 10 feet.[12] In the morning following a cool, dark night, the winds usually subside, and the water remains calm until the sun warms the air. However, by early afternoon, the expanding and rising hot air creates a wind, which can be dangerous to canoes and small boats. When the wind

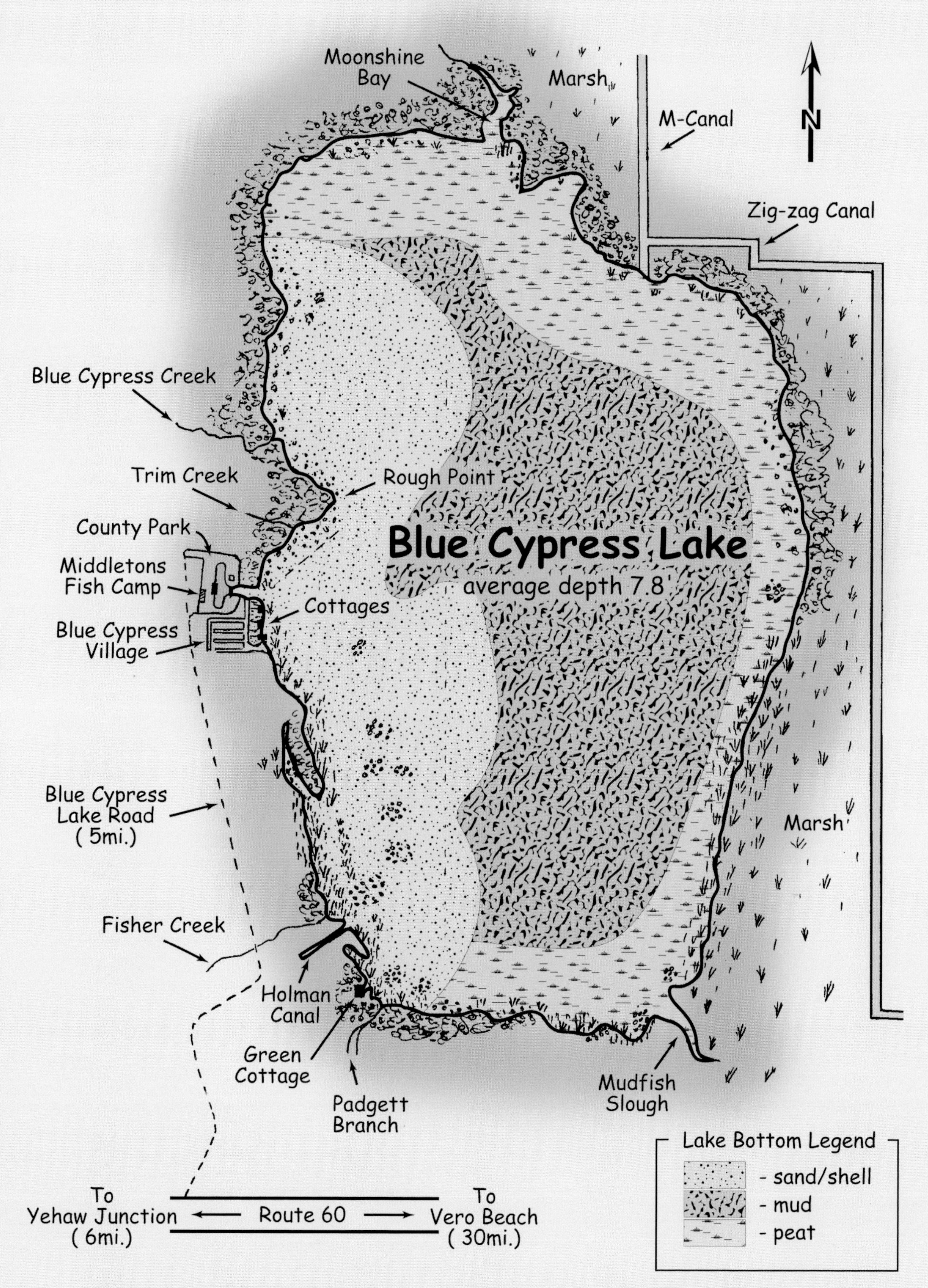

Figure 3. Map of Blue Cypress Lake indicating major features, sediment types, and major inflows on south and west and outflow of the M canal (modified after maps drawn by Carl Faxon and Warren and Hohlt[105]).

blows, the lake's shallowness and large size can cause large whitecap waves to build quickly and surprise the unwary angler or sightseer, especially those in small boats. A number of people have drowned on the lake. In less than seven months between 1983 and 1984 four people drowned,[5] and others have died in recent years.

THE BOTTOM LINE

Fine sediments cover 81 percent of the lake bottom at an average sediment thickness of 4.9 feet.[12] On the lake's west side (Figure 3), bottom sediments, composed of coarse sand have a very low organic content which increases towards the east and northeast sides of the lake where the organic muck and peat accumulate up to nine feet thick. The thickest sediments (15 feet) are located along the northeast shore where cypress trees extend out into the lake.

In Blue Cypress Lake, the food chain begins with the leaves, flowers, fruits, and seeds serving as a major food source for zooplankton and bacteria, which in turn are eaten by aquatic invertebrates that are then eaten by fish, amphibians, reptiles, birds and mammals. The peat material on the eastern edge contains and holds the nutrients, which are slowly released for use by wetland plants. This contrasts with upland forests, where the vegetation is more easily exposed to air and is decomposed under higher nitrogen and oxygen conditions, resulting in the nutrients being readily recycled rapidly back into the forest food chain.[57]

The sand sediments on the western shore support a rich community of species such as clams and immature mayflies. The biological mud communities in the middle of the lake and peat on the eastern edge are less diverse and contain species known to tolerate conditions of low dissolved oxygen and accumulated decaying organic matter such as segmented worms and midges.[105] The aquatic invertebrates distributed throughout the lake include 46 species of non-biting midges, 15 species of segmented worms, 7 species of snails, clams and mussels, and 6 species each of dragonflies and mayflies. Compared to Lake Okeechobee, Florida's largest lake, which is more polluted, Blue Cypress Lake supports greater numbers of bottom dwelling (benthic) species across all habitats and a greater number within each individual habitat.

The two most common bottom dwelling invertebrate animals found are the native burrowing mayfly and the exotic Asian clam.[105] The clam was purposely introduced into British Columbia during the 1920s and first noticed in northwest Florida in the 1960s. This bivalve develops faster than native mussels because it does not have a larval form that requires a fish host, as do most native species. This helps it out-compete the native species.

Mayflies are not only found in May but throughout the spring and summer when they emerge periodically as adults in huge numbers at Blue Cypress. First appearing in the fossil record 350 million years ago, mayflies belong to the order Ephemeroptera meaning short-lived (ephemera) and winged (ptera). The immature naiads feed on algae, other tiny plants (phytoplankton), and small aquatic animals, and they may live as long as four years before becoming adults.[66] The naiads have specially flattened forelegs to form a scooping shovel and their jaws appear as projecting tusks, which they use to tunnel along the bottom like underwater moles.[96] At night they emerge from water as gill-breathing juveniles (naiads), much like fish, but, in less than ten seconds, they are transformed into air-breathing flying adults. Most usually die before dawn. Some live a few days, but they do not feed as adults. Their stomachs are only filled with air and their mouthparts are much reduced after evolving from generations without use. During the night, after emerging as adults, many thousands of males, with their translucent, veined wings, fly up and down together in a sensuous dance. When females enter the male swarm, they too join in the dance until a male seizes them. Then they fly away for a few minutes of sexual union. Within an hour, the fertilized females lay their eggs, attaching each by short filaments to aquatic plants. Then they die. All is not wasted, however, as dragonflies, spiders, fish, and birds, particularly the swallows, feast on the dead and dying adults after they emerge from the naiad stage. It is ironic that these short-lived individuals have survived on this planet for hundreds of millions of years!

In contrast to other lakes, Blue Cypress has aquatic invertebrates (mayflies, amphipods and grass shrimp), rather than forage fish, as the primary food source for sport fish (bluegill, redbreast sunfish, redear sunfish, black crappie, and largemouth bass).[105] The black crappie, for example, is totally dependent upon invertebrates for food in both juvenile and adult stages. Thus the fishing success at Blue Cypress greatly depends upon the health and prosperity of the mayflies, amphipods, and grass shrimp. Their presence indicates ample phytoplankton and detrital food sources, low turbidities, and adequate concentrations of dissolved oxygen. Any major decrease in the density of invertebrates would signal a shift in water quality, which would adversely affect the food web of the lake. If, for example, there were high water levels for long periods of time, the population size of nearly all invertebrates would be reduced, while deep-water (less desirable) species would likely increase. Therefore, controlling the water level is important in order to maintain invertebrate biodiversity and fish production.

The rust brownish color of the water is the result of tannin (tannic acid) and other organic or humic acids coming from slowly decomposing surrounding vegetation forming peat and humus under wet acidic and low nitrogen and oxygen conditions.[57] However, the surface of the water reflects the sky, and on a sunny day, the lake lives up to its colorful name. Viewing the lake at different times of day and beneath different clouds reveals a variety of colors ranging from sky blue and gray to the reds and oranges of the predawn, as our photographs depict.

THE "REDWOODS AND SEQUOIAS" OF FLORIDA

The lake's shoreline and adjacent wetlands support such plants as sawgrass, maidencane, willow, spatterdock, alligator flag, red maple, swamp tupelo, redbay, and sabal palm. With the help of Janice Broda, former president of Florida Native Plant Society, a list of common plants found at or near Blue Cypress Lake is provided in Appendix I. However, the signature tree of Blue Cypress Lake is the giant bald cypress, towering 70-120 feet above the lake surface and growing hundreds of feet into the lake from the shoreline. They are the "redwoods and sequoias" of Florida, standing alone like majestic noble sculptures in a huge water park. In fact, cypress trees are in the same family as California's redwoods and giant sequoias (Taxodiaceae). These trees were probably the same age, 500-600 years old, as the largest old growth stand of virgin bald cypress still preserved in Audubon's Corkscrew Swamp Sanctuary. Their age make them the giants they are, and cutting even one is a tremendous and irreplaceable loss of a majestic antiquity. Further out from shore, the cypress trees are dwarfed or have stunted foliage due to limited nutrients, constant inundation and/or wave action. These trees, only 10-12 feet tall, are very old and are nearly as large in diameter at the base. Being both conifers and deciduous, these trees change during the seasons with leaves turning from green to reddish brown. Even dead cypress trees reveal a subtle beauty. Their weathered forms appear as sculptures. Trees with bare branches, perhaps damaged by lightning, give the effect of dancing ballerinas pirouetting as we glide by. When the branches lose their needles in the late fall, many more join the dance.

Cypress trees have interesting peaked structures often called "knees" for their worn bareness on top and hair-like bark on the sides growing around the base of the trunk. They arise from the root system and protrude above the water or ground, all around the tree, 2 to 5 feet or more away from the trunk. There are various theories to explain why these knees exist. Knees range in height from barely visible to nearly three feet tall. One old theory suggests that they help aerate the tree's root system, but the removal of the knees seems to have no apparent impact on the vitality of the tree.[72] Cypress trees are known to be stable and strong in high winds and their large buttressed base appears to support them. Interestingly, the trunk bases are often completely hollow; sometimes they terminate just below the water surface and do not even contact the earth.[72] Perhaps the knees, being a part of the root structure, play a crucial role in propping up the tree, especially in storms.

A number of plant and animal species make cypress trees their home. Growing on or in the hollow of these trees, we have found sabal palm, pond apple, strangler fig, tupelo, red maple, hickory, primrose, dog fennel, rose pluchea, salt bush, poison ivy, moonvine, white vine, air plants, climbing asters, resurrection fern, golden polypody fern, Boston fern, Brazilian pepper, and marijuana although the last was in three pots wired to the tree! When hollow and dead, the cypress are perhaps the favorite nesting sites for the brilliant little yellow prothonotary warbler, sometimes referred to as the "swamp canary." It calls a simple, but loud and penetrating, *tsweet, tsweet, tsweet, tsweet*. Howell recorded it breeding at Padgett Creek near the lake.[43] The many holes and cavities in the cypress trunks are also home for the ever-present woodpeckers, as well as the great crested flycatchers, wood ducks, eastern screech-owls, black-bellied whistling-ducks, various water snakes, and raccoons. In addition to calling distinctively, the pileated and red-bellied woodpeckers, drum loudly on the trunks. Drumming is done to attract a mate or define its territory. The limbs provide nesting and/or perching sites for screeching hawks, bald eagles, peregrine falcons, owls, warblers, anhinga, herons and egrets, ibises, vultures, and many other migratory bird species. A list of other common birds we found around Blue Cypress is provided in Appendix II.

At the base of the cypress trees, we frequently find the limpkin, a species closely related to the rails, named for its "limping" walk of lifting a foot high with each step and twitching its tail with an upward jerk. Limpkins are fairly tolerant of being photographed and are often seen walking around the Fish Camp and Blue Cypress Village. During the day, we hear them calling loudly *kur-r-ee-ow, kur-r-ee-ow, kr-ow, kr-ow* or knocking shells to get snails.

The Florida apple snails are Limpkin's staple diet along with frogs, worms, insects, crustaceans and other mollusks. The apple snail's egg clusters, commonly found on the cypress knees, trunks, and other wetland plants, are generally laid between March and July. They become mature reproductive snails in 12 to18 months and die a few weeks later after laying their eggs.[15] Snail kites in the marsh feed nearly exclusively on apple snails. White ibis, boat-tailed grackles, alligators, redear sunfish, and soft-shelled turtles prey on them as well.[15]

"Grand Ole" Osprey

What claims center stage on the magnificent cypress trees? It is the osprey, with its sharp shrill call *tewp, tewp, tewp, teelee, teelee, tewp*. The cypress trees, large and small, provide ideal nesting sites for a large population of ospreys; a nest can be found about every 100 feet in cypress areas during the breeding season. Perched on a cypress limb, overlooking the water, these fishers from the sky keep an eye out for fish (their only food source), for crows (which prey on their eggs), or for other ospreys (who show off their fish as they circle, screeching, and competing for their space). We counted 158 active nests around the lake one January 2002 day. Osprey breeding season begins in November at Blue Cypress and lasts until July. Breeding ospreys come from South America and other areas in Florida. Some remain here year-round, particularly males who may be guarding their nests. There may be influxes of northern populations of ospreys stopping to feed and rest while others continue on to South America in the late fall and return in early spring.[54]

During the 1950s and 1960s, drastic declines in the osprey, peregrine falcon, brown pelican and bald eagle populations provided the crucial evidence that DDT caused thinning of their eggshells. Because they were big birds, "you could not miss them, and when you did miss them you knew something was wrong."[37] DDT was banned in the United States in 1973, and since then populations of ospreys, peregrine falcons and bald eagles have been making significant recoveries, and all three species can now be found at Blue Cypress. Humans, however, are still dealing with DDT: we still have it in our fat, and there has been a suggested link between testicular cancer and DDE, a DDT breakdown product.[37]

Ospreys, a.k.a. "fish hawks," are included in the same family (Accipitridae) as the medium-to large-size diurnal raptors (hawks, kites and eagles), which have hooked beaks for tearing flesh and strong legs and sharp talons for grasping, holding, and sometimes killing their prey. Over the last fifteen million years of evolution on all continents except Antarctica, ospreys have fine-tuned their successful fishing expertise. Ospreys have spiked scales on the bottoms of their feet and one reversible talon that enable them to grab slippery fish, which they then take back to a tree perch or nest to eat. Their eyes have a transparent, protective membrane allowing them to see while diving. The black feathers around their eyes help them to reduce glare from the lake's surface. This bandit-looking mask is much like the eye-black that athletes smear on during games.[37] Being a superb athlete, the osprey hunts fish by hovering up to 100 feet over the water and then plunging head-first at speeds of over 40 miles per hour towards the water, at the last moment swooping their talons into the water to capture a slippery, scaly creature. Then immersed, the osprey must get out of the water with a fish weighing nearly half as much as itself. Besides having great strength, the long, high-arching wing design allows the osprey to carry much heavier loads in relation to body size than any other bird of prey. After shaking off the water and turning the fish's head forward to reduce air drag, the osprey continues flying almost effortlessly. This is done several times a day during its entire life, depending on the number of mouths to be fed.

Osprey nests at Blue Cypress are bulky and in various states of disrepair. The nests are three to four feet in diameter and two and a half feet tall, and made principally with sticks. They are generally built on top of cypress trees, whether large or stunted. The male brings large sticks and branches used for nesting material, and the female builds, guards, and lines the nest with bark, moss, and small sticks.[94] Two or three eggs are normally laid, and they have a 34 to 40 day incubation period. At hatching, the chicks are protectively feathered with soft down, have open eyes, and immediately begin feeding by sight. The male does most of the fishing for the entire family, while the female generally stays in the nest, feeding and looking after the chicks for the next two months. Learning to fly and catch fish takes an additional 4-8 more weeks. Young ospreys first seem to jump up in the nest flexing their wings. Their first flight has been described as wobbly with uncertain wing flaps and a seeming certain crash into the lake, but they recover and climb high above the lake, gliding in circles and practicing steering and control.[38] Then they begin to follow their dads on fishing trips.[94] They learn to catch fish before leaving the Blue Cypress Lake area in late fall and heading for northern South America. The one-year-old birds remain in South America for the first summer; not until they are two years old will they return to Blue Cypress to build their own nests.[94]

Canoeing on Blue Cypress Lake

If you wait until 10 am you miss a lot,
the changing light, the active birds;
the sun is hot, the UVs are strongest,
and often the winds are picking up.
We once considered crossing the lake
but decided against it
because winds can kick up
without warning,
forming white caps making it too risky
to cross in a canoe.
By 1pm the waves sometimes are fierce.
We struggle to keep from being swamped
from hitting hidden logs and stumps.
Best time is early morning,
when the waters are likely to be calmer.

There are two sunrises
if we are lucky
to have clouds high in the sky.
Taking our chance this will happen today,
we awake when it is very dark,
making coffee while
readying our gear,
then slipping our canoe into the water.
Early, before the sun breaks the horizon,
it shines on those high clouds
the whole Eastern half of the sky becomes
brilliant, deep reds and oranges.
These gradually fade, darken,
the sky is dull,
then suddenly the second sunrise begins,
brilliant rays hit clouds at the horizon,
the orange edge of the sun breaks out
reflecting across the water.
Clouds in front of the sun are edged in gold.

Pennywort, perky
rhythmic row,
necks stretched
all facing east
towards the glorious
sunrise
...front row seat
through time.

Treasures

Anywhere one can get away
to as large an area as this
and savor little pockets of Nature's beauty,
undisturbed...
These are treasures...
Rare.
They must be preserved.

Peacock butterfly-
common in the tropics

Green treefrog-
active in evening
with a cowbell-like
quaink in chorus
with different pitches

Tricolored heron

Water lettuce
jewels glistening in the sunshine.
No other plant here allows the water to collect
in plump balls like gems catching the light
and sparkling just for us
as we pass.

After just a few hours on Blue Cypress
we can return to the battlefield of our chosen work...
to try to repair the trauma of sexual abuse,
to preserve the natural landscape and habitats so future humans can learn and enjoy,
to educate students to strive for excellence, integrity, and humanity,
to work to reduce discrimination, bigotry, and intolerance;
to insure rights and basic needs of health, welfare, and education;
and to raise funds to train others to work with these problems,
for the benefit of the whole world.

Blue Cypress Lake stretches wide and far
such an expanse of sky!
No human construction visible aside from the base fish camp...
which in a matter of minutes is out of sight.
Quickly immersed in this wilderness,
sometimes with drama as the waves suddenly rise,
the clouds darken and wind becomes fierce...
more likely quietness,
disturbed only by the calling of the birds,
flitting of dragonflies,
the jumping of a fish,
the plop disappearance of the turtle slipping off its log,
or the alligator being startled as it dozes in the sun.

A mile away

Even though they may be as much as a mile away,
we turn our heads in their direction,
towards the very center of the Lake
when we hear the wing beats and noise from the landing of a huge
flock of ducks.
It is difficult to identify them without a telescope,
we agree that some of them look like lesser scaup.
We remember the old timer's story of hunting wood ducks here,
Stuffing the beauty, now darkened with age,
to hang on his cabin walls as trophies to his exploits.

Memories of the hectic city life
Office politics, sexual innuendoes,
little maneuverings, angst, strivings
...steps to glory
...concerns that nag, pondering of problems...
yet the lapping of lake water,
fragrance of star flowers,
flitting of butterflies
restore the ideal
what really is important...
the fullness of the moment.

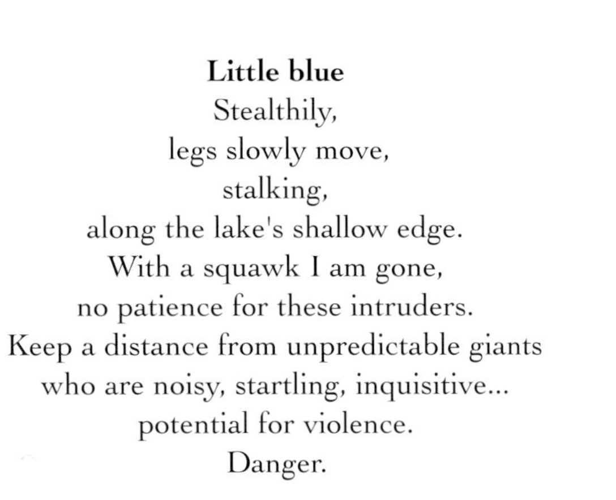

Little blue
Stealthily,
legs slowly move,
stalking,
along the lake's shallow edge.
With a squawk I am gone,
no patience for these intruders.
Keep a distance from unpredictable giants
who are noisy, startling, inquisitive...
potential for violence.
Danger.

Juvenile

Adult

Blue Cypress Creek's plant covering makes it appear as a manicured lawn

Marsh mallow

Queen butterfly
Male possesses brushes on the tip of their abdomens that during courtship release a compound that subdues the female during mating.

Native red hibiscus

Look carefully
Or you'll miss easily...
The dragonfly darting,
the marsh mallow blooming.
The red of the Florida holly or native hibiscus
peaking through;
the butterflies quickly moving flower to flower.

Listen! What sounds are those?
The pileated woodpecker announcing his presence,
the osprey's persistent call,
the flapping of the vulture's wings,
the Carolina wren's melodious voice
opening the hammock to music,
the motor boat drowning out
the cardinal's "tsks."

The woodpeckers have been busy on this tree!
None here now though.
What little critters/delicacies were they finding?
When was it? How many years ago?
Will they ever return?
Are the particular ones who enjoyed this tree still alive?
Where might they be now?
How many nesting seasons were here?
How many of their babies have survived?

Viceroy

Pickerelweed

Turn on your sniffer
get close to the fragrance of the white vine
take deep breaths of the fresh air, so pure,
but ignore the distinctive smell
of the passing boat's gasoline.

Spatterdock

Breathe Deeply
the smells brought by the wind,
lost in one's contentment...
the vast expanse of the sky
and lovely beauties
make those images of "our other life" vague,
giving needed perspective,
enabling a return to the battle.

Entering Middleton Fish Camp at 10 P.M.
it is quiet, the tackle store is closed,
everyone is in their tent or trailer.
We pull into a spot in our handy little camper van,
Our bed folds out and is made in a minute.
We lie in the dark,
the stars are brilliant here,
falling stars easy to catch during celebrated showers.

Listening to the night sounds....
coming in our screened windows with the cooling breeze.
The repetitive croak of the tree frog,
the flop of a fish in the canal right beside us,
the deep throated 'frump' of an alligator,
'who cooks for you?'
calls the barred owl-melodious and hollow.
Yet our ear is jarred by
the drone of another camper's air conditioner...

Barred owl

Mysteries of the forest-remains of the last giants

Fleeting moments...
Sunlight ever changing
bird on a wing,
wind blowing water
in patterns never the same
found sculptures decaying
new growth sprouting
catch the beauty now!

Each sunrise is distinctive
offering a new and different color spectrum,
different cloud patterns.
Which way shall we paddle?
north or south?
to find the tree or a protruding branch
that is most artistic.
Which will look most extraordinary,
bold and dramatic,
silhouetted against the sunrise?

Every visit, a new phenomenon-
This morning thousands of swallows flying low, flying high...
all flying in the same direction...
North, coming from the south...
yet this is fall and they must be migrating from the North...
Always puzzles we would love to ask knowledgeable scientists.
Of course, maybe they don't even know.
There are still plenty of unanswered questions
in this world.

Spores on the
giant leather fern

The world from Blue Cypress
seems manageable,
simple, a microcosm one can understand.
Far away from war, terrorism, violence against women,
child abuse, pettiness, and passions...
although the outside world sometimes intrudes
even here...
the jet stream cuts across our sunrise,
the drone of an airplane,
"ta boom!" the distant guns hunting,
the roar of a pontoon boat.

Spanish moss- epiphyte of the South

So easy to destroy
so long to create.
Evidence of once giant cypress as the huge
6–7-foot diameter cut stumps remain.
In the 85 years since the great cutting,
None of the current living trees are as large,
none worth harvesting...
oh yes, we discover a few magnificent trees
tall, straight, and proud
on the far side of the lake.

Practicalities

Although in emergencies we have
teetered on the edge of our canoe
to find a foot hold amongst roots and bog
to stand and then to balance precariously
making sure no boaters are around
to watch our private act,
we would prefer not to risk
polluting the lake,
tipping the canoe,
running into poison ivy
or getting our feet wet.
Since there are no camping
or toilet facilities
except at the launch site,
our longstanding habit has been
to stay out only 4-5 hours.

Yet we yearned to explore all around the lake.
Would it be different over there?
Are we missing wildlife and habitats?
What mysteries, beauties, might we discover?
We knew that, to create enough time to cover
the roughly 16 miles indicated,
to investigate every corner, stream and bay
and to photograph every interesting plant and creature,
along the way,
we needed a whole day.

Designs in nature-swamp tupelos

The day we choose to paddle around the lake
turns out to be in January, very foggy, but magical.
Being enveloped in a cloud heightens the drama.
As we set out, the dark shapes of partially emerged stumps,
looming cypress, and quiet persons fishing glide past us.
We had wanted to capture all weathers, at all light levels,
this is our opportunity.

Circumnavigating the lake

Cypress trees are dense,
standing in the water, majestically,
as we start out.
Periodically we pass stumps of cypress,
long ago harvested.
As we paddle past each live tree,
the ospreys sitting on their nests,
start crying out,
"Chiii! Chiii! Chiiii!"
waiting until the last minute,
flying up as we get too close,
circling, scolding in protest.

Moonshine Bay

On the north and northeast side
the cypress thin out
and are more likely to hug the shore.
Blue Cypress Lake flows into
the wide M Canal at the northeast side.
This water does flow to the sea, eventually.
Rounding the east side,
we catch sight of a spotted sandpiper
flitting from log to log
just ahead of us as we progress,
never standing still to let us pass by.
The cypress trees are smaller here,
interspersed with small bushes, and lake grass.
We stop for lunch, insuring our canoe is in the shade
of one of the few cypress trees
Soon even these disappear
and we find ourselves in an open marsh area
with not even a backdrop of cypress trees or hammock
and no osprey nests.

Then in the distance,
in some higher trees,
the osprey nests begin again.
Soon, beautifully isolated trees
appear in the water and,
when we reach Mudfish Slough
(really flowing from Fort Drum Creek) in the south,
we feel we are actually going to make it around the lake today.
By now, we have taken 6 rolls of film
and have enjoyed a very lovely day.
Our worries that the wind will pick up in the afternoon are groundless.
The afternoon is even calmer than the morning,
with a glasslike water surface reflecting the bright blue sky,
the snowy white clouds,
and many wildlife wonders still to observe.
By the end of our adventure around Blue Cypress Lake,
we have counted 158 osprey nests.
Our final bird count is 38 species.
A marvelous day.
We've made it back around to the west side,
waiting to watch the sunset.
Almost 12 hours in a canoe.
...stiff...
but we did it!
So this is our favorite place,
see why we want to share it with you?

Grand Ole Osprey

Marvel at the cycle of life...
Nest building, courting, chasing,
stealing fish, dropping fish, diving for fish,
exclaiming over their territory.
Protecting young, raising fledglings,
scaring others away,
screeching in protest.
Leaving,
nests falling apart from disuse and storms,
cypress turning fall colors,
the sun rising and setting.
The Osprey...will go on for centuries,
Long after we live our lives.

Cypress changing colors

Tiger swallowtail and bee on buttonbush

Art from many angles of one tree

Lovers

Red maple

We are drawn to investigate
inside the hammock,
going in and out
from under the cypress trees.
Spotting drift wood,
discovering the iris or lily blooming
in a corner infrequently visited.

Entering underneath the dripping canopy
we hear a chorus of black and white,
yellow-rumped and yellow-throated warblers,
and much activity from Blue-gray Gnatcatchers.
Nearby, a Phoebe sits motionless
as he waits for a tiny prey,
then darts from his branch and back again.

As we paddle deeper inside the trees,
we discover a green-back heron
sitting so silently, watching.
Not minding our getting close,
seeming to know we are confined to the canoe
and can't harm her,
giving us permission to take her picture.

We come upon a tree
with such beautiful golden lichen
growing on its trunk
a stark contrast to the surrounding leafy green...
These little discoveries
make us eager to see
what is around the next tree...

Swamp lily

Alligator flag

How is it macho?
to crush beer cans
and scatter them
wherever one is?
Must we,
the apple snails, bass,
the alligator
have to view them...
in the amber clear
water reflecting
the sun
streaming
by?

Green heron

Limpkin

Over a decade

Although we have been coming here for over 12 years,
some things we observe are rare...
Timing is everything.
An apple snail laying eggs. The mayflies swarming.
The barred owl sleepily eyeing us from a near branch.
The baby gator sunning on the log,
keeps slipping off, and climbing back up to watch us.
The whistling-ducks standing in the tree, no,
clinging to the high bare branches
with their bright orange webbed feet,
yes, whistling!

Apple snail laying eggs in early morning

There you are!
Long before seeing them,
the Limpkin certainly
makes its presence known
either with its characteristic squawk or
the sound of cracking the shells of apple snails
to retrieve the tasty fleshy morsels.
Let us join you,
we'll have breakfast too,
while we watch you,
here in our canoe,
but from a different menu.

Turkey vulture

Apple snail eggs
on red-stemmed
alligator flag

Mysteries of the swamp...
where do the hundreds of vultures come from?
How do they get enough to eat?
How far do the ospreys travel when they're not hanging out at Blue Cypress?
How many hundreds of years have the ospreys been nesting here?
What birds used to inhabit Blue Cypress, but no longer?
Did the Indians live self-sufficiently here on this lake?
How? What plants did they eat?
We see numerous egg rafts, but where are the baby snails?
What factors have led to this lake being preserved,
largely untouched,
when most others have attracted swarms of humans?

Animals in habitat-romantic imagery
creates a sense that all is right with the world,
that Eden is still out there,
that the idyllic will last forever.
Humans have in fact destroyed
much of the world's original habitat
in a relentless search for
farmland, living space, lumber, minerals...
to accommodate 6 billion humans...
...900 species endangered,
1000s already destroyed...
wildlife preserves...
where ecology is controlled by humans
rather than by the interaction
among animals, plants and earth
...separate the truly priceless from the meaningless
...are these "objects" of exquisite formal beauty
worth saving?

Double-crested cormorant

Whither the water?

On a hot day, I plunge my hand
deep into the cool water.
Ripples of water flow around my hand,
making graceful patterns as we pass by.
I cup my hand and let the water pour out.
Eventually this water flows North out of the lake.
Where will it go?
From these headwaters down the St. Johns River,
out through Jacksonville.
Will it be caught up by the Gulf Stream and
then flow North and across the Atlantic Ocean?
To Africa? And then?
I am connected to you,
to everyone in this world
by the flow of water,
by what each of us does to this water,
right here, wherever we are.

Black Vulture

An amazing sight...
hundreds of
black and turkey vultures hanging out in the trees,
crowding together on every available tree limb,
with their wings akimbo,
spreading their feathers to dry.
Congregating and carousing with their kind...

As we come upon them all around us in the tops of trees,
we stop paddling,
we are silent, watching, not disturbing...
For awhile, they don't move,
and then suddenly,
all at once and for no apparent reason,
(delayed reaction to our presence?)
they take flight,
flapping their huge wings
and heading out in all directions,
nearly running into each other,
using sudden avoidance maneuvers.

In our fast paced
media centered,
automobile confined
consumer oriented,
populated malls,
hectic fast food eating
era....
the walls of humans' inhumanity
seem to be closing in...
we hear of murder, rapes, domestic violence, sexual sadism...
but here is peace, seeming safety,
reminding us of ancient times
when life seemed simple.
There are few spaces like this left
in the once vast Florida wilderness.

Alligators...
aren't you scared in that little canoe?
We have canoed and swum in many lakes and rivers...
it is only scary when we suddenly come upon alligators...
And they discover us too close!
Alligators like to sleep in the sun...
canoes make very little noise.
Alligators aren't used to humans coming up silently...
Don't be in their way as they desperately flee!

But if they see you first,
they are curious...and immediately sink into the water,
keeping their distance,
but always watching you
with just their eyes and nose above water.

Yellow crowned night heron adult

Juvenile

What a surprise
as we enter a glen
which at first seems like any other.
We see a yellow-crowned night heron
sitting on a branch, oh, there's another.
As we get closer,
our presence scares up one, then another,
only then do we spy them in their flight,
but we get better at spotting them
as they sit motionless,
blending in with the gray branches...
There must be almost two dozen
gathered in this one special meeting place
amongst the trees.

Oh, look, a peregrine falcon!
sitting in one of the huge tall cypress trees,
not flying up like the ospreys do,
even though we have come very close.
She's so preoccupied,
picking at her distinctly beautiful feathers
with her long,
bright yellow talons

We love the birds
As we paddle,
we explore the ins and outs of the trees,
following bird calls,
each one having its own special voice.
Amazing.
We know who they are just by listening,
often not being able to see them at all.
Trying to make as little noise as possible,
we get as close as we can to the birds
to photograph them
either standing before us
or perched high above us.
The anhinga and great egrets
silently fly away as we approach,
but ospreys, herons,
and most birds loudly protest
or frantically flee.

We marvel at the patterns of their lovely
feathers,
plumes blowing in the wind,
and their grace.
We are intrigued
with their antics and unique behaviors.
Through binoculars,
their beauty is revealed.

Anhinga

Found sculpture-
capture the moment,
as they are never the same.
The scene changes with...
the sun behind the cloud,
the time of daylight,
water height and wave action,
wind,
plants growing around them change the artistic effect...
still a beauty,
but a different work of art...
dramatic and artistic.

Photographs preserve
long after my memory fades.
Yet how difficult to capture
the dramatic waves in a storm,
the sticky, steamy, summer heat,
the wonder of the clouds
catching the changing light,
or the absolute peace of still waters.
My feeling at the picture's instant
is also affected
by what I have been experiencing this week,
always by the person I am with,
or the thoughts I am having
at this very moment.
But the photograph
can bring back these feelings
and evoke others in those
who have never had the privilege
of sharing this particular moment with me.

10 years later,
all that is left

May, 1996

February 2002

Changing light
of the sun's colors alighting on objects,
requires close observation.
In the early morning,
trees glow red then yellow.
The sun illuminates the tupelo and cypress trees
with an inner warmth and energy.

. ...late morning sun is luminous,
late afternoon casts shadows...
clouds often cover the sun,
just as we are set to take a picture...
wait for the sun, patience.

Cree, cree, cree!
urgent cries
from the top
of the kingdom,
Red-shouldered hawk
puts us on
alert

Anhinga-upper left

Summer

Winter

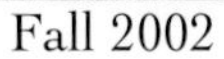

Fall 2002

Winter 1991

What colors?

Sunrise brilliant hues of oranges, red, purples,
fog grays to variations of black,
bright summer shades of greens,
winter's rust browns,
the deep dark blues of the night sky,
pink, yellow, green, gold, orange,
reds of the tree lichens.

It is still a thrill
to pick out the familiar pair
of bald eagles circling high
in the thermals,
majestic wings spread,
white head and tail flashing as they turn,
near the spot where we had seen them
on another day.
Then the pair had sat surveying the lake,
near the tops of the trees,
not moving
hardly visible to the untrained eye.
We wonder if they will nest here this year.

Around the world, and here in Florida
beauty like this has been eliminated, replaced, obliterated...
with cottages, skyscrapers, cement, manicured lawns, and repetitive golf courses.
Paradise paved over.
How unique this is to have escaped! The swamp around has served it well.
The legislatures of the state of Florida have seen this vision and provided
matching funds to communities to preserve natural lands like this.
Thank you Indian River County citizens, county commissioners, land acquisition committee,
and St. Johns Water Management for your time, monies, and commitment.
In ten years there will be no land left to preserve.
America has always been so amazing...we thought we would never run out of open spaces.
And to think this all could have been developed.
Hopefully from our sharing our pictures and thoughts,
you can glimpse reason for our passion.

IF ONLY THE CYPRESS COULD SPEAK—HISTORY OF THE LAKE

OUT OF AFRICA

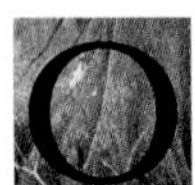

Originally, Florida was under the sea. Florida's basement rocks, Osceola granite and various high-feldspar volcanic rocks, lie 1-3 km (0.6-1.8 miles) beneath the surface and were formed in the Cambrian Period (600 million years ago), the earliest stage of the **Paleozoic** Era.[106] These rocks along with similar **Paleozoic** fossils and the magnetic orientation of the iron crystals embedded in these rocks suggest Florida separated from part of West Africa (Gondwanaland) and was joined to North America in present-day Georgia at the beginning of the **Mesozoic** Era (225 million years ago).[106]

TIME LINE OF ERAS...YEARS INDICATE WHEN ERA STARTED YEARS AGO (NOT TO SCALE):

PRE CAMBRIAN ERA 4.5 BILLION YEARS	PALEOZOIC ERA 600 MILLION YEARS	MESOZOIC ERA 225 MILLION YEARS	CENOZOIC ERA 65 MILLION YEARS AGO TO PRESENT
INVERTEBRATES			
	FISH		
	LAND PLANTS		
	AMPHIBIANS, INSECTS		
	REPTILES		
		DINOSAURS	
		BIRDS	
			MAMMALS
			APES

About 25 million years ago in the **Cenozoic** Era, Florida began to rise from the sea, and for millions of years, its size and shape changed from smaller to more than twice its present size with corresponding climate changes from mild to tropical and wet to dry depending on water levels.[13] Fossils found in rivers, springs, and sinkholes suggest grassy savannahs, which provided rich browsing for horses, camels, and even rhino-like rhinocerotids and long necked giraffe-camels.

TIME LINE IN FLORIDA (NOT TO SCALE):

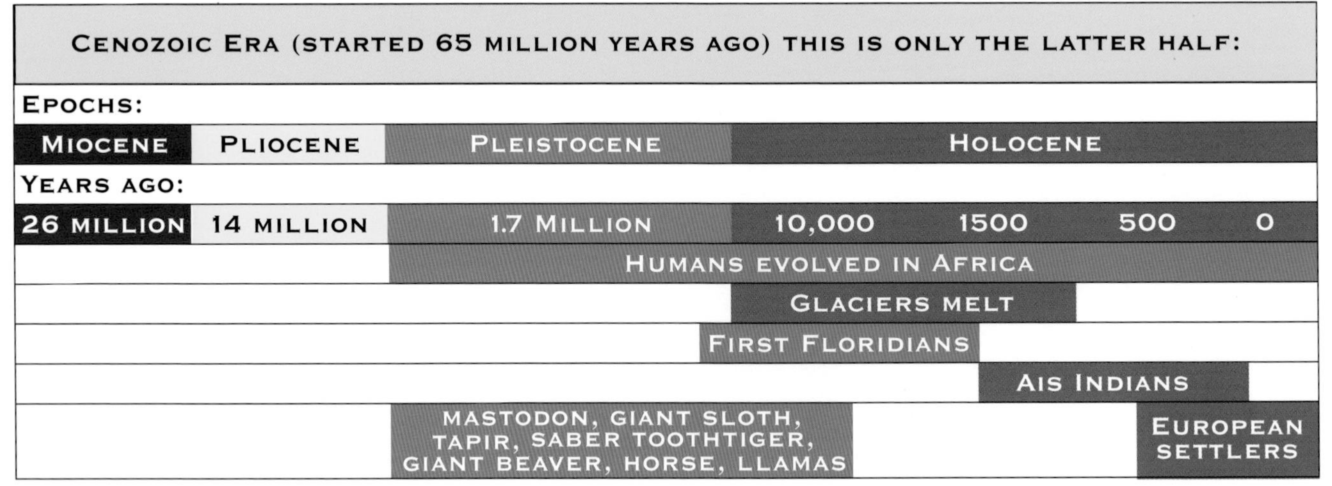

Historically, water flowed into Blue Cypress Lake from the west and south from the marshes and small creeks, and then exited by sheet flow toward the north. The five other lakes of the Upper St. Johns River differ from most lakes found farther inland in that each is elongated in the direction of the river flow, with the inlets and outlets at the opposite ends of the lakes. This is true regardless of the orientation of the lake. Other Florida inland lakes, however, have different shapes, groupings, and orientation in relation to drainage. Their inlets and outlets appear random and are not necessarily at their ends. This arrangement supports the theory that the lakes in the Upper St. Johns River Basin are remnants of a long brackish, or perhaps freshwater, estuary separated from the ancient ocean by a chain of barrier islands,[110] much like the present east coast of Florida. The alignment of upper basin lakes along the mainstream of the river and the presence of sediments between the six lakes suggests that they are remnants of this continuous body of water and became isolated due to sedimentation during several different periods of high sea-levels.[110]

During the first half of the ■Holocene Epoch, around 10,000 years ago when humans were present, the interior of Florida was relatively dry. Evidently lakes like Blue Cypress would not have been as large. Approximately 5000 years later, a gradual rise in water levels within a few meters of present day levels produced Lake Okeechobee and the Everglades[41] and probably the outline of the present-day St. Johns Marsh. However, southern Florida probably did not reach its present topology until 2700 years ago.[41]

WHAT WAS BLUE CYPRESS LIKE A MILLION YEARS AGO?

he first fossil evidence of mammoths and mastodons was found in the early 1900s during the digging of the first drainage canals east of Blue Cypress Lake. A few early fossil vertebrates, including Columbian mammoths and American mastodons, were found in or on the ■Pleistocene Epoch shell marl.[84] In 1993, Jennifer McMurtray, a land manager for the St. Johns River Water Management District, discovered additional fossils from the same time period (around 0.6-1.4 million years ago) about five miles northwest of Blue Cypress Lake at the Tucker Borrow Pit. Investigating this site, paleontologists Gary Morgan and Roger Portell,[69] describe over 1,000 vertebrate fossils representing at least 50 species that were found including 4 species of sharks, a ray, a sawfish, 10 species of bony fish, a frog, 9 species of turtles, an alligator, 3 species of snakes, 4 species of birds, and 15 species of mammals. These indicate that Blue Cypress Lake was a shallow, near-shore salt water marine environment.

Fourteen of those 50 vertebrate species are now extinct, including two land tortoises, the giant ground sloth, the giant beaver, horse, llama, bison, mastodon, and mammoth. The presence of the giant tapir and the mammoth indicate that the vertebrate fauna were present during the early to middle ■Pleistocene. The invertebrates, consisting of mostly marine mollusks, were abundant in the late ■ Pliocene Epoch. The presence of the freshwater and terrestrial fauna suggested to Morgan and Portell that "a river flowed into the Atlantic Ocean near where the fossil site formed, carrying the bones of the freshwater and terrestrial species into the shallow marine environment where they were deposited."[69]

Another site, twelve miles east of Tucker Borrow Pit along the north and south banks of the Sebastian Canal (C-54), was examined in 1967 and 1968.[6] Twenty-five species of vertebrates, similar to those at the Tucker Borrow Pit, were found. Of the 13 species of mammals found there, ten are extinct.

Cypress trees that are now dominant at Blue Cypress Lake were also common during the ■Pleistocene in Florida, as demonstrated by the seeds and cone scales found in extensive swamps 12 miles west of Vero Beach.[6] The DNA of fossilized cypress twigs recovered from a ■Miocene Epoch lake deposit in western Idaho was nearly identical to the DNA of modern cypress.[40] Thus, the namesake tree of the lake, "cypress," may have survived many environmental changes during the 26 million years of its terrestrial history.

To get an idea of additional plants present during the ■ Pliocene and ■Pleistocene Epochs, we can look at the digs around Vero Beach roughly 30 miles east from Blue Cypress Lake. Archaeological activity in Vero Beach began in November 1913 with the discovery of fossil bones in the Main Relief Canal near the Indian River Lagoon. In October 1915, Vero Beach briefly became the "Mecca" of Florida paleontology with the discovery by Mr. Frank Ayers of the remains of what was perhaps a late ■Pleistocene human, called "Vero Man", in the bank of the same canal 512 feet from the Florida East Coast Railroad.[85, 89] Many animal fossils were found in the same layer as Vero Man. One was a new tapir species, later named after the place where it was found (*Tapirus veroensis*). Fossilized plants common then (and most, even today) at the Vero sites were slash pine, red maple, pond apple, loblolly pine, sedges, cabbage palmetto, wax myrtle, cork wood, saw palmetto, muscadine grape, viburnum, sweet or swamp bay, and gallberry. Interesting corkwood is now found only in North Florida, which suggests that the climate in Vero Beach was somewhat different then compared to now. Also in Vero Beach, fossils of the following birds were found: turkey vulture, tree duck, herons, barn owl, gull, terns and egret.[87]

FLORIDA'S FIRST SNOW BIRDS

When glaciers covered much of the earth and the seas were lower towards the end of the Pleistocene Epoch about 12,000-15,000 years ago, humans crossed a land bridge from Siberia to Alaska and spread south throughout the Americas including Florida.[10] While much of North America was covered in ice and snow, peninsular Florida offered a gentler climate with above-freezing winters and cool summers because it extended into the Caribbean. However, as the glaciers melted and the sea level rose, Florida was reduced in land area by about half, and the vast loss of xeric and open habitats must have also decreased the megafauna during the late Pleistocene.[106] The first people in Florida hunted, gathered plants, and fished, but had no knowledge of pottery. They made baskets, built shelters, and fashioned tools of bone, chert, and wood. Later, about 4,000 years ago, some of the first clay-fired tempered pottery, using palm fibers and Spanish moss, appeared along the St. Johns River.[10]

The first Floridians lived alongside the elephant-like mammoths, giant armadillos, saber-tooth cats, huge wolves, and land tortoises, as well as present-day animals such as deer, rabbit, black bear, raccoon, opossum, panther, and bobcats,[107] many of whose fossils are found near Blue Cypress. The sea level then was 320-380 feet lower than today, and Florida was much drier than at present.[62] Rather than flowing rivers, there were probably watering holes, perhaps Upper Basin lakes, that attracted both humans and other animals. Large mammal and early human (Paleo-Indian) interactions are documented by a skull from an extinct bison found along the Wacissa River in Jefferson County, Florida, that had a fragment of chert from a projectile point intentionally driven into it. Radiocarbon and biostratigraphic dating place the age of the bison at about 11,000 years.[107] Bison also once grazed near present-day Vero Beach. [108]

In 1929, the distinguished paleontologist and evolutionist George Gaylord Simpson, writing about the extinct land mammals of Florida, gave the following poignant statements that seem true for today's humans, who are continuing to cause massive extinctions of species around the world:

> "The final chapter in the history of the animal life of Florida, that of transition from Pleistocene to recent times is a disastrous one....The present fauna of the state is only the poor and colorless remnant of that which it once supported. Half, or perhaps even two thirds, of the Pleistocene mammals are now extinct and those of their companions which still survive are not only relatively few in numbers but are also generally the smaller and less striking forms. The rabbits, squirrels, rats, mice, some of the carnivores, and one of the deer have survived, but the sloths, armadillos, horses, tapirs, camels, mammoths, mastodons, and many others no longer exist. It is not possible to assign a definite cause to this decimation, but if present conjectures as to the antiquity of man here prove to be correct, it will seem quite probable that the destruction of animal life by man, still going on, started with his victory over some of the Pleistocene mammals, a victory for which one must now feel some regret."[89]

Robert Weigel carried out extensive fieldwork at the Vero Beach site during the summers of 1956 and 1957 with the assistance of John Beidler, then Director of the Indian River Mosquito Control District.[108] Weigel supports the theory that humans were present at Vero Beach and Melbourne during the extinction of typically Pleistocene animals and may have been responsible for their accelerated demise. Most all of the extinct forms at Vero were large and would have been easy targets for predation by humans. Mass extinctions have been noted in New Zealand, Polynesia, Australia, and Madagascar soon after the arrival of humans.[111] Not only were animals killed for food, but also the habitat changed so that plants and countless small animals perished as well. This accelerated the demise of the Pleistocene animals. Support for this theory comes from DNA collected 100 feet into the Siberian permafrost from mammoths, bison, and dozens of plants which suggests that roughly 11,000 years ago the environment made a sudden shift from a landscape of mostly herbaceous plants to that of shrubs and mosses.[83] These scientists and others believe that it was environmental change and not just human hunting that was responsible for the demise of large mammals.

Sadly, however, the pattern continues today. According to the Union of Concerned Scientists, we are changing the climate through increases of anthropogenic greenhouse gases.[103] Our continued population growth also modifies and destroys native habitats. More recently, Carolina parakeets, ivory-billed woodpeckers, and passenger pigeons all have been wiped out. The first two used to be present at the Blue Cypress Lake area. The Carolina parakeets officially became extinct in 1904, but a flock of about 30 were seen on nearby Fort Drum Creek in February, 1920 by Henry Redding, a person "who knows the birds well."[43] The demise of the Carolina parakeets was also in part due to their social nature. "If one is accidentally wounded, the others hover around the injured one until sometimes the whole flock is exterminated. This devotion to one another has cost them dearly, and many thousands have been destroyed in this way."[43]

The ivory-billed woodpecker, the largest woodpecker in North America, was huge (19-21 inches long). It made 14-36 inch cavities, 30-50 feet high in living cypress trees, for nesting and roosting. In addition to the attraction of its ivory bill, hunters must have found them very tasty as "the crackers consider them better than ducks!" according to Arthur Wayne in 1893.[43] The last one seen in Florida was probably in February 1924 in the Upper St. Johns River Basin at Lake Poinsett by D. J. Nicholson. Their sounds, like the "burry reed notes of a Scotch bagpipe,"[43] probably will not be heard again.

DISCOVERING HUMAN TRACES ON BLUE CYPRESS LAKE

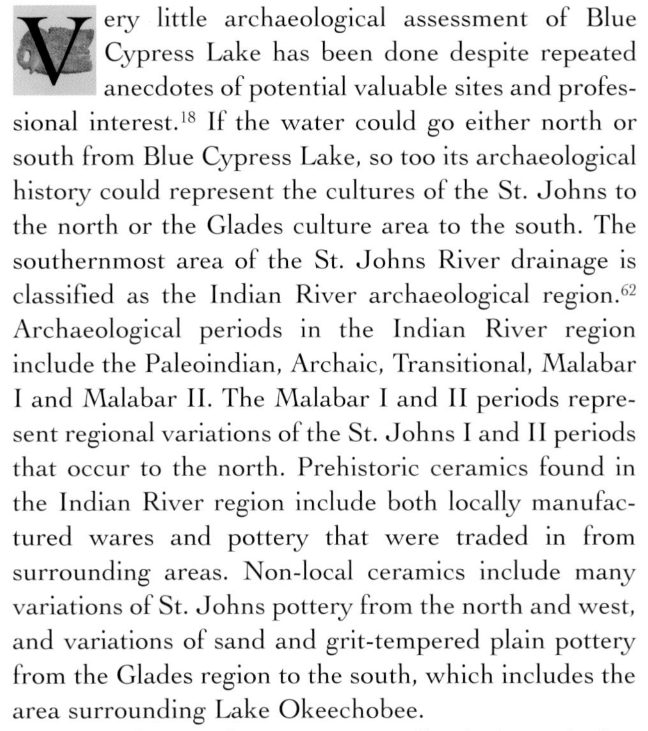

Very little archaeological assessment of Blue Cypress Lake has been done despite repeated anecdotes of potential valuable sites and professional interest.[18] If the water could go either north or south from Blue Cypress Lake, so too its archaeological history could represent the cultures of the St. Johns to the north or the Glades culture area to the south. The southernmost area of the St. Johns River drainage is classified as the Indian River archaeological region.[62] Archaeological periods in the Indian River region include the Paleoindian, Archaic, Transitional, Malabar I and Malabar II. The Malabar I and II periods represent regional variations of the St. Johns I and II periods that occur to the north. Prehistoric ceramics found in the Indian River region include both locally manufactured wares and pottery that were traded in from surrounding areas. Non-local ceramics include many variations of St. Johns pottery from the north and west, and variations of sand and grit-tempered plain pottery from the Glades region to the south, which includes the area surrounding Lake Okeechobee.

A submerged site, Faxon-Holland, (named after Carl Faxon, a local bass fisherman and supervisor at Piper Aircraft and James Holland who discovered the site) located a quarter mile into the lake may have very important middens and fiber-tempered ceramics preserved in stratified deposits. A site report[19] based on W.A. Cockrell's 1966 notes and information from Faxon and Holland describes Paleolithic lancet-shaped projectiles (possibly 12,000 years old), Early Archaic points (9,000 years old), and Late Archaic/Transitional period Orange Plain Fiber Tempered Pottery (4,000 years old). Apparently two skulls, one human and one dog, were also discovered near each other that may be more than 10,000 years old.[55]

If true, this would place human occupation of the lake margin around the same time period as Vero Man described above. Artifacts from earlier dives including arrowheads, pottery and sharks' teeth indicate at least three eras of Indian tribes lived in the area. Sonny Cockrell, Florida's State Underwater Archaeologist, is quoted as saying that the Faxon-Holland site is "one of the most significant sites in Florida" and "could turn into a major archaeological project."[55]

The underwater Faxon-Holland site indicates that the water level of the lake once was lower and thereby smaller in area than at present. This would be expected 11,000 years ago during the Pleistocene Epoch because the water levels were much lower than now. The presence of cypress trees projecting into the lake also suggests lower water levels for at least part of a year because cypress seeds do not germinate underwater. Thus the cypress trees in and around the lake may be very old. Peat formation on the lake's eastern shore likely made the lake deeper over time (Figure 3). Dickel reports that the submerged site may be a well-preserved stratified resource that could document change through time. Thus the bottom of Blue Cypress Lake may be an important source of hidden knowledge of early inhabitants.

During the drought of 2002 and low water levels in 2003, we found a number of thin potsherds lying on the sandy surface near a spit of land on the western shore south of the county park where the water had receded. Some of the pottery pieces are shown in Figure 4. Scott Mitchell at the Florida Museum of Natural History in Gainesville, FL identified 95% of them as plain, gray-black, and undecorated Sand Tempered ware. Sand Tempered pottery was made over a long period of time from 500 B.C. to 500 A.D. These potsherds were thus made at least 1,500 years ago. Due to the different rim construction of several pieces, a few might be Belle Glades Plain which Native Americans began making about 200.A.D. A few smooth pieces were St. Johns Chalky Plain Ware made during the period 500 B.C. to 800 A.D. Also from this period we found one larger seemingly unbroken clay artifact, unusually shaped with a hole in it. This could be a worn potsherd, a manufacturer's by-product (irregular lumps of clay), children playing or, as we speculate, an amulet! No stamped or incised potsherds (made only after 800 A.D.) were found. Alongside all of these ancient pottery pieces was historic pottery called White Ware with a pearl glaze made in the 1700s to 1800s, which could have been used up to the early 1920 to 1940s by white settlers or Seminoles in the area.

Figure 4. Potsherds from Blue Cypress Lake. Top two rows: Sand Tempered, third row: St. Johns Chalky Ware Plain, fourth row: possible Belle Glade Sand Tempered, fifth row: White Ware and a piece of porcelain.

David Dickel, currently the Florida's State Archaeologist, briefly describes in his 1992 report the discovery and cursory search of a major prehistoric freshwater shell midden in a mound under the old Holman Lodge (Blue Cypress Lake Lodge) near the southwest corner of the lake. Although no marine shells were found, freshwater mussel shells were extremely abundant. Throughout the shells were traces of what the Indians ate: bones of small fish (catfish and others), turtle, bird, snake, small alligator, amphibian and deer. The pottery suggested Belle Glade and St. Johns Plain types. Dickel guessed that "the site appears to be an occupation hamlet or small village used repeatedly but probably not permanently."[18]

These three sites and other unconfirmed reports indicate that the western shore of the lake may have had extensive early Indian settlements, especially near the mouths of Blue Cypress Creek, Padgett Branch, and surrounding areas which may have been submerged most of the time. Unfortunately, Dickel indicates that ranch property owners west and north of the lake did not give access to carry out field tests to confirm the high probability of archaeological areas.

The Ais Indians and Their Demise

What was life like for the native Indian population living on Blue Cypress Lake? Although we do not know much about the people who left the potsherds at Blue Cypress, Irving Rouse[81]and recently Robert Davidsson[16] provided extensive historical information on the Ais Indians who were the Indians present when Europeans arrived. Before 1700, the Blue Cypress Lake area was probably used for hunting by the Ais Indians of the St. Johns River who were related to, but thought to be separate from, the main tribe of Ais Indians along the Indian River Lagoon.[81] Based on artifacts found along the St. Johns River, Blue Cypress Lake was at the crossroads of a cultural exchange between the Timucuan tribe to the north and the Calusa to the south.[4] However, the Ais were fishers, hunters, and gatherers rather than farmers and were related linguistically and culturally to the Calusa and other tribes of south Florida.[81] Dugout canoes made from the slash pine were probably their primary means of transportation, using wooden paddles in open water and long poles in marshes and tidal flats.[16] Belleville[3] speculates that the Calusa, who lived in the Everglades, could paddle their cypress dugouts up the Shark River Slough into Lake Okeechobee and then northeast across Allapattah Flats, following the water-saturated streams such as Fort Drum Creek that meander north to Blue Cypress and the St. Johns River to the ocean at Jacksonville.

The Ais diet probably consisted of fish, turtles, and alligators, as well as deer, raccoon, snakes, waterfowl, and small game.[16] Hunters used thin throwing spears, fish weirs and cast nets to capture fish. A number of plants growing in the area were gathered and eaten, such as palmetto berries and cabbage palm (swamp cabbage). The shell mound or midden, with its accumulation of thousands of discarded shells, upon which the Holman Lodge was built, indicates they also enjoyed eating numerous freshwater clams. Potsherds indicate they were advanced pottery-makers with a variety of vessels for holding food. In addition to spears, the Ais warriors used clubs and bows and arrows. The arrowheads were made of bone, shell, or animal teeth. The adult Ais were taller than the average Europeans. The men wore loincloths made of Spanish moss or fiber and the women wore deerskin or woven material, with their long hair rolled up atop their heads and held by a carved bone pin.[16] Perhaps the leader of the tribe who lived on Blue Cypress Lake lived on top of the shell midden near the edge of the lake, as was customary in the area.

Before the arrival of Columbus, Florida was a very different place from what we see today. There were no drainage canals, dikes, dams, built-up roads, or permanent bridges. There were no infectious diseases such as smallpox, scarlet fever, typhus, typhoid fever, diphtheria, cholera, chicken pox, measles, and influenza. Christopher Columbus describes the first Indians he saw in the Antilles, "There is not in the world a better nation. They love their neighbors as themselves, and their discourse is ever sweet and gentle."[60] Although Columbus recognized them as friendly, generous people living in harmony with their environment, within 10 years these people had been slaughtered, enslaved, and driven to extinction. Certainly diseases, especially smallpox, did play an important role in the extirpation of other North American Indian tribes.[60]

In 1700, Father Alonso de Leturiondo, a Florida native, noted, "Florida is of so admirable a climate, of so beautiful a sky that for men's health no equal to it has been seen."[16] However, early residents had to tolerate numerous mosquitoes, sandflies, and other biting insects. Apparently, people believed that it was not unusual for chickens to be killed by exsanquination by female blood-feeding mosquitoes. Many years later, Walter Kitching "tells of two railroad workers found dead one morning under a water tower. They apparently had gone to sleep, sodden with alcohol, and were 'murdered' by mosquitoes. Their bodies reportedly were swollen to twice the normal size."[99]

Mosquitoes were more than just pests. In Florida,

over 10 species of *Anopheles* mosquitoes are capable of transmitting the malarial parasite to humans. Malaria is a very ancient disease described by Hippocrates in the fifth century B.C. Recent genetic evidence on malaria clones estimate that it originated 100,000 to 180,000 years ago.[71] Malaria in humans is not just one disease but is caused by four different species of protozoans. Over 100 similar but different parasite species are found uniquely in other animals. This high host specificity also indicates a long association between the four parasites and humans. Malaria probably developed in prehistoric humans as they first evolved in Africa and has accompanied us throughout our evolutionary history.[42] How malaria established itself in the New World is subject to much speculation.[1] One theory is that malaria did not exist in North America prior to the European colonial settlements but was introduced by the Spanish, English, Dutch, and French or was brought in via the African slaves by the Spanish. Others suggest that some malaria species traveled with the early humans when they crossed a land bridge from Siberia to Alaska and spread south throughout the Americas including Florida and Blue Cypress Lake.

Before 1500, there may have been as many as 100,000 native people in what is today Florida; however, by 1800, only 250-300 years later, after imported diseases and harsh treatment from European invaders, all original Floridians were gone.[10] The Ais apparently did not succumb to the missionary's attempts at conversions or the political control of the Spanish following the arrival of Ponce de Leon near St. Augustine in 1513. Although there were contacts, they were not always pleasant or peaceful.[16]

The extinction of the Ais began in 1690 when the northern Indian tribes in Georgia (Yuchi, Oconee, Creek, and Cherokee), usually led by the British, began raiding the Spanish missions. Davidsson gives a detailed description of the final demise of the Ais.[16] A possible reason for the attacks was that the cultivation of maize and beans had exhausted the Oconee soil in Georgia. One attack in 1703, led by Captain T. Nairn of South Carolina, extended as far as the Ais territory in the headwaters (perhaps up to Hell'n Blazes) of the St. Johns River.[30] By 1763, these repeated attacks, and perhaps the introduction of smallpox, other diseases, and alcohol, had nearly exterminated the Ais. There is some evidence that a few of the Ais may have taken refuge among the fierce Calusa (who killed Ponce de Leon in 1521 on his second trip to Florida and also finally perished themselves) in southwest Florida. A few of the Native Americans then traveled on to Havana, Cuba, where they perished, bringing an end to the habitation of Florida by this indigenous population.[41,95]

The extinction of the large animals and even the Ais and Calusa of our *Homo sapiens* species should be a chilling and sobering lesson for us. Extinction rates of all species have intensified throughout the last century and are now the highest ever, and still rising. If this human caused destructive trend continues, 20% of the current species will be extinct by 2030, 50% by the end of the century.[111] Many species are not yet even identified, and we are losing them. Blanchard so eloquently makes a similar point with regard to the disappearance of the Ais and Calusa, "The loss of their wisdom and knowledge stopped 12,000 years of tradition in its tracks, causing an informational implosion, a thunderous silence that continues to echo through the Native American world today."[7] The world has lost their centuries of gathered knowledge of herbal medicines native to Florida, their language, folk songs, crafts, stories, poems, and their agriculture practices. Today, there are remnants of the mounds and villages Native Americans created, but we are guilty of removing even these reminders to build railroads and roads, or covering them up with buildings, strip malls, and parking lots that are built to accommodate our relentlessly growing population.

SEMINOLES

After the demise of Florida's first people by 1763, a new Native American group moved into Florida, with its center on the St. Johns River. The Seminoles, whose name means "exiles" or "runaways," were formed from the invading Oconee and Creek Indians of the north reinforced by other Indian and Black slave fugitives from the Spanish and British colonies.[95] Although the British established trading posts on the St. Johns River, they and the Spanish, who regained control of Florida in 1783, left the Seminoles alone. Thus, the European presence was largely confined to the coastal areas of the Indian River Lagoon. The Seminoles inhabited the Upper St. Johns basin, perhaps including Blue Cypress Lake and probably were not affected by the First Seminole War (1816-1818) in North Florida.

Even after the purchase of Florida by the United States in 1821, the Indian River Lagoon and the Upper St. Johns River remained isolated and largely unexplored. Not until the Second Seminole War (1835-1842) brought troops to Central Florida were these areas more fully investigated. This war was an attempt to remove the Seminoles to Oklahoma so white settlers could occupy the rich Florida farmland. In 1838, General Jessup led an expedition against the Seminoles from the navigable headwaters of the St. Johns River to the Jupiter Inlet along the eastern edge of the Everglades. During this war, Army posts were temporarily established at Fort Taylor on Lake Winder, Fort Vinton (southeast of Blue Cypress Lake), and Forts Capron and Pierce on the Indian River Lagoon.[81] After the war, not all the Seminoles were removed to Oklahoma, and some drifted back to the Lake Okeechobee area, including one group that came to Blue Cypress Lake.[90] Joe Carroll (personal communication, Aug. 2003), working for the US Fish & Wildlife Service, found evidence of their presence near Fort Drum Creek. Ruth Stanbridge (personal communication, Sept., 2003) has confirmed their presence.

HIDDEN LAKE

Why did it take so long for the lake to make it onto the map? During the Seminole Wars and after the period 1839-1885, a series of at least 13 military and plat maps of the Blue Cypress Lake Area surprisingly do not show the lake. An 1839 military map (and some of the later maps) labels the general area of Blue Cypress Lake "Cypress Swamp" with no distinct boundaries. Interestingly, however, this map shows two streams labeled "Chitto Hatchee" and "Arta Hatchee" (hatchee meaning creek or river) placed in the same general area where Blue Cypress Creek and Padgett Branch, respectively, are found today. Humans traveling up the St. Johns River probably stopped at Hell'n Blazes, because there was no permanent open natural channel further south to Blue Cypress Lake, only a vast marsh.

Even on the 1884 map, which detailed the major and minor lakes of the area, including Lake Washington in Brevard County, Blue Cypress Lake was not noted, although an active military trail going south to Fort Drum passes just three miles west of the present shores of Blue Cypress Lake. Since the trail crosses Blue Cypress Creek, it is surprising the creek was not followed to its destination to reveal the lake. According to Ruth Stanbridge,[91] the trail was blazed during the Second Seminole War (1835-1842) under General Eustis's command west of Blue Cypress Lake and south to Fort Drum. Remnants of this trail in Indian River County are still used south of State Road 60 and north of the Fellsmere Grade (Fellsmere-Kenansville Grade).

Could the Indians have kept it hidden from the military? Unlikely. Could the lake not have been there, due perhaps to a long period of drought or changed water flow? In contrast to some lakes formed by geological processes or dam building, Blue Cypress Lake and the surrounding marsh was formed by a biological process. If water is pumped out of either Blue Cypress Lake or Marsh for agriculture or other reasons for extended periods of time, the peat soils on the east side (Figure 3) would become dry (Paul Gray, personal communication, Jan. 29, 2003). The soil would then start to decompose by oxidation, and even worse, fires could start and burn, and the peat would disappear even faster. Over time, the marsh and lake could drop to lower levels and might disappear, as we know them, not being able to recover. Both the peat soils and Blue Cypress Lake need each other to form and survive: the lake relies on peat soils to hold its water in, and the peat relies on the lake to keep it wet. Therefore, the thriving peat and large lake is evidence that it existed then. Even today, we need to be careful not to drain it too long or too low, otherwise it will really disappear.

An official detailed 1885 map of Brevard County, which at that time also included Indian River, St. Lucie, and Martin Counties, made by J. Francis Le Baron, C.E., Deputy U.S. Surveyor, gives us a clue as to why the lake was not mapped. All land on this map, except for a cluster of 5 townships, had been surveyed, including Lake Washington. The 5 unsurveyed townships had no details; across the blank space was written "UNSURVEYED, IMPASSIBLE MORASS". Two of the western-most "unsurveyed impassable morass" townships included Blue Cypress Lake and one of the eastern townships included Fellsmere. As a result of the canals, much of the surrounding area has been drained for farming, and today it does not appear at all to be like an impassable morass.

THE LAKE IS "DISCOVERED" AND ON THE MAP!

When Florida became a state in 1845, the Federal Government transferred most of the land to the state government. Much of this land was then sold with little or no thought to the future. There was no plan defining how communities might be best designed for humans to live together or how to preserve the beauty of the land and habitats for wildlife to thrive. In 1890, the Trustees of the Internal Improvement Fund, who were responsible for the sale of state-owned land, sold four of the five unsurveyed townships for 50 cents an acre, was sold to Mathew R. Marks, Cecil G. Butt, and Willis L. Palmer of Orange County.[98] However, the partnership was unable to make all payments, and in 1895, the entire tract ownership of

115,000 acres was transferred to Mr. Anthony Octavius Russell, a printer and president of the United States Printing Company of Cincinnati, who wanted to develop it.

Interestingly, besides buying and developing land, Russell's printing company printed theatrical and circus posters, placards, labels and playing cards. The playing card business became very successful and was separated from the parent company in 1894. It became the United States Playing Card Company, one of the largest playing card makers in the world. We know them for the "Bicycle" and "Congress" card decks which have been in continuous production since the 1880s. The latter is the deck of choice for sophisticated bridge players.

In 1895, Russell immediately hired Orange County Surveyor John Otto Fries, Deputy Surveyor S. A. Robinson, Arthur T. Butt, and Chas. E. Rinaldi to survey the 5 remaining unsurveyed townships. The Fries survey team left Orlando on April 23, 1895, to survey the immense saw-grass ponds at the head of the St. Sebastian and St. Lucie rivers. After being in the "Impassible Morass" for six weeks, the team "discovered" a lake, roughly 4 miles long by 2 miles wide, in the midst of a broad prairie.[44] The surveyors returned to "civilization" by hitching a ride on a new freight train that ran from Titusville through Sebastian to Vero. Henry Flagler had built the Florida East Coast Railway in 1893-1894 through the eastern part of the county after retiring as John D. Rockefeller's partner at Standard Oil.[50] This allowed easier access for development. Mr. Fries then went right to work to prepare a correct map of the tract.

THE MYSTERY OF TWO NAMES

The resulting 1895 "Cincinnatus Map" by Fries, so called because Russell referred to the land as the "Cincinnatus Farm Land Project," is the first map to show Lake Wilmington (the original and perhaps still the "official" name for Blue Cypress Lake) as a lake and not a cypress swamp. In an undated letter (probably after 1900) kept at the Florida State Library, Tallahassee, Fries describes the area:

> "On the west side (of Russell's property) is located Lake Wilmington, about 4½ miles long, and 2½ miles wide. North of this lake is located the famous 'Blue Cypress.' The west boundary line runs north through this swamp, leaving a little more than one half outside this property. I estimate that there must be at least 1200 acres of first class cypress on this property. The trees stand very close together and are uncommonly tall and of great diameter, of first class quality."

Surprisingly, the lake described by Fries is in nearly the same shape and nearly the same size as current maps. Moreover, from Fries description, the area north of Lake Wilmington was apparently known by the locals as "Blue Cypress" because of the cypress trees, which some have described as having a similar color as those in the Blue Ridge Mountains of eastern United States. Others say that in the moonlight the cypress trees look blue. The creek leading into Blue Cypress Lake on the west side was also called Blue Cypress Creek on some of the early maps.

Pamela J. Cooper, Supervisor of Indian River County Main Library's Florida History & Genealogy Department, on a tip from Bob Gross, researched how the lake got it's first "official" name. Most likely the lake was named after a member of the Wilmington family in Cincinnati. Perhaps it was Russell's mother's family name or his cousin, James Willis Wilmington, also a printer. James Wilmington, along with his wife, Frances and family, shared the same household with the Anthony Russell family, according to the 1860 Cincinnati census. Both Anthony and James enlisted in the Union Army on the same day, April 20, 1861, Anthony as a Captain (age 34) and James as a First Lieutenant (age 20). Both served in the Ohio 6th Infantry Regiment. Anthony survived the war leaving as a Major and field officer, while James, a Captain of Company B and later Company C may have died in the Civil War or shortly afterwards. Company C of the Ohio 6th Infantry Regiment saw fierce battles at Shiloh, Tennessee and Chickamauga, Georgia. The 1870 Cincinnati census listed only Frances Wilmington and not James, and even she did not continue to live in the Russell's household according to the 1880 Cincinnati census. Anthony also had named one of his sons, Willis, perhaps after James Willis Wilmington. However, it is still speculation and a mystery why Russell may have thought it appropriate to name it Lake Wilmington.

Why and when the name was changed to Blue Cypress Lake is unknown. A Fellsmere Water Control District Plat Map, dated January 28, 1920, labeled the lake for the first time as "Blue Cypress Lake." Other towns and area names were changed around that time too, perhaps to appeal to tourists and buyers. For example, Quay became Winter Beach. Even today, some government maps have its original name, some give both, but most maps and locals now call it Blue Cypress Lake, which certainly is descriptive, because on a sunny day, the lake looks blue and is surrounded by majestic cypress trees.

Major Environmental Impact on the Lake by Humans

In the second undated letter in the Florida State Library, Tallahassee, Fries also wrote that of the 115,000 acres surveyed, 70,000 had 4 to 6 feet of muck on top of clay and marl and 20,000 acres had less muck. On the far eastern side, a portion of about 1500 acres of the remainder was covered with low pineland and numerous ponds and grassy marshes. The Fries survey crew determined the elevations from the lake to the Middle Fork (West Prong) of the St. Sebastian River, a distance of four or five miles, and determined that there was a 20-foot fall, "ample to enable the entire tract to be drained at comparatively little cost." This was later estimated to be about $300,000.[45] Russell's plan for draining his land was to make a dike around the west, south and north boundaries, leaving out the lake and Blue Cypress area. According to Fries, Russell was also going to dredge a canal to furnish an outlet for Fort Drum Creek and all the numerous creeks flowing into this marsh. Finally, a main canal was to be cut from the eastern edge of the marsh nearly due east to the St. Sebastian River, a distance of about four to six miles, and going over the 700 foot wide Ten Mile Ridge which they estimated to be six to ten feet above the marsh. Fries felt that there was "no large tract in this State better fitted and more apt for successful cultivation of sugar, rice and other products than this tract." The lake was intended to be used as a reservoir to water the crops in times of protracted drought. Fries speculated that the land would soon be worth $50-100 an acre.

The lake and surrounding area were now ripe for development. Only a few weeks after the lake's discovery, Mr. Russell's son, Willis W. Russell, who was involved with the day-to-day running of the Cincinnatus Farms, was reported to advertise for bids for "cutting necessary canals to drain the lands...to proceed with the work of drainage as rapidly as possible."[44] A few months later in 1896, Russell laid a ten-mile spur from the Florida East Coast Railway in Sebastian to the eastern edge of his property, called the Sebastian and Cincinnatus Railway.[48] Ninety-five African Americans cut the 20,000 railway ties for the spur from trees of the nearby woods.[46] The *Indian River Advocate* speculated with enthusiasm that a surveying party would continue to survey the route on to Tampa![49] A relic of the spur line can still be found at the northeast corner of the intersection of Indian River County Roads 510 and 512.

While the spur never made it to Tampa, Fries was elected as Brevard's County Surveyor.[47] As one of the state's earliest surveyors, Fries surveyed much of Florida including parts of the Everglades, and in 1900 he took the first census of the Seminole Indians. He died in Orlando in 1931 at the age of 93.[2]

Land Development and "Let's Drain Florida"

Originally, half of Florida was wetlands, but by 2002 over half of the wetlands had been drained for agriculture, flood control, and residential development.[78] At the time of Russell's purchase, state-owned lands were being sold and the proceeds were used to fund the "improvements," which meant draining the lands. On maps today, state land is marked "TIIF," meaning the "Trustees of the Internal Improvement Fund," which is the Governor and Cabinet who own it in trust for the benefit of all Floridians. Land development in Florida was encouraged by Governor Napoleon Bonaparte Broward, elected in 1905, who mobilized the state's resources to reclaim the Everglades by constructing drainage canals to "allow surplus water to drain off into the Atlantic Ocean and Gulf of Mexico."[74] He and his successor, Albert W. Gilchrist, spent nearly $2 million of state funds on this ambitious and environmentally disastrous plan. By 1913, 142 miles of canals and two locks were in place in the Everglades.

Fell's Mere

Implementation of grand "reclamation" schemes was not limited to draining the Florida Everglades. Russell died in 1900 before any other development occurred, and his family unable to carry through with Russell's plans sold the land in 1909 to Mr. John J. Heard, who in turn sold it to Mr. E. Nelson Fell in 1910.[88] Fell, a retired English mining and hydraulic engineer, believed that private enterprise could do a better job than the state had done in the Everglades and that it was possible to drain the Blue Cypress Lake area and sell the land for a handsome profit. He bought the 115,000 acres plus an additional 3,000 acres of the pristine prairie, marsh, and woodlands starting from seven miles west of Sebastian to the east side of Blue Cypress Lake for $1.35 per acre and formed the Fellsmere Farms Company.[74] The name "Fellsmere" was a combination of the founder's name and the English word "mere" which means a small pond, lake, marsh or "a great watery place." A few years later some of the same land was sold for $100 per acre as Fries had predicted.[3]

In 1911, with the financial backing of the wealthy

Virginia engineer and entrepreneur Oscar T. Crosby (who later became an Assistant Secretary of the Treasury under Woodrow Wilson), Fell and his engineers dredged the largest gravity-based drainage system in Florida. It consisted of a Main Canal connected to an Outlet Canal, 5 lateral canals, and a series of sub-lateral canals for agricultural production and private development.[74] Four colossal excavators began opening the twelve-mile Main Canal. This marked the beginning of physical and hydrological alteration of the floodplain around Blue Cypress Lake, primarily to support agriculture. The Main Canal was constructed across the marsh north of Blue Cypress Lake from Fellsmere to the lateral M Canal, and the resulting dike or levee was part of the Fellsmere-Kenansville Road. All excess water from the five lateral and sub-lateral canals would eventually flow eastward from the Main Canal to the Outlet Canal, which flowed into the Middle or West Fork of the St. Sebastian River and to the Indian River Lagoon (Figure 5).

On February 21, 1912, the *Fellsmere Farmer*, the Fellsmere Farms Company newspaper and promotion document, compared the Main Canal to the Chicago River, which was reversed in direction from draining into Lake Michigan to eventually going into the Mississippi River.[31] The paper boasted:

> "In both cases engineering skill, money and the excavator turned the trick against the order of nature. Instead of the waters of the Fellsmere plateau flowing sluggishly with 23 or 24 feet fall for a hundred miles or more down the St. Johns River course, it gets that same fall in less than six miles to tidewaters of the Indian River. What could now prevent nature itself from effecting a perfect drainage for the Fellsmere lands through natural erosion?"

The same issue indicated that Lake Wilmington would be lowered by four feet when the drainage system was completed, which would have reduced the lake's volume by 50 percent.[12]

After the first eight thousand acres were "reclaimed," settlers arrived almost immediately from the Midwest eager to try their luck at the headwaters of the St. Johns River. By June 1912 Fellsmere had a population of 600 and was the second largest town behind Ft. Pierce in St. Lucie County, which at that time included Indian River County.[74] St. Lucie had broken away from Brevard County in 1905.

Figure 5. Artist's rendition from a 1912 Fellsmere Farms Company development promotional document showing the proposed draining of Lake Wilmington and surrounding area via the M Canal to the Main Canal, Outlet Canal, and Middle Fork (West Prong) of the St. Sebastian River into the Indian River Lagoon. (Photo reproduced by Clarence F. Korker from the collection of Rodney Tillman).

Blue Cypress Lake and Broadmoor Get Platted

On June 26, 1913, the *Fellsmere Farmer* announced that the dredge named St. Lucie had entered Lake Wilmington to drain the wetlands around the lake.[32] The headline read, "From Lake Wilmington to the Atlantic Ocean–Water flowing through Fellsmere Canals to the Seas." Directly on the eastern shore of the lake were platted 64 separate lots for development into lakeside cottages. Luckily, the wetlands around the lake were never sufficiently drained, and cottages were never built. This area of the lake remains undeveloped. In October of 1913, another town, called Broadmoor, five miles west of Fellsmere and only a little more than two miles northeast of the lake, was completely platted for sale with 9 business blocks, 57 residence blocks, 2 parks and a railway station.[33] It was slightly smaller than Fellsmere, occupying three-quarters of a mile square versus one-mile square. Some northern truck farmers started to farm and live in Broadmoor in the winter, and then move back north to farm in the summer.[101] Many families lived in tents and shacks and had no time to build houses.[100]

Raising Cane

A 1913 sales brochure for Fellsmere Farms described efforts to grow sugar cane in the area.[73] In the following year, a new settler from Illinois, Robert Kann, announced his intention to plant forty acres in cane and erect a large syrup mill two miles west of Broadmoor, near the northwest shores of Lake Wilmington. However, Kann's attempt at cane production failed and the mill was never built.[73] The lake was spared again. Charles H. Piffard, President of the State Bank of Fellsmere and longtime friend of Fell's when both had worked together in Siberia, tried to raise a variety of crops including sugar cane and an excellent long fiber cotton. However, the boll weevil and expense of picking rendered his venture unprofitable.[102]

Yeehaw

According to the *Florida Star* (November 27, 1911), another major western extension of the Florida East Coast Railway was started to "push steadily into the very heart of the Everglades and opening to the world for development a new empire of fertile lands and magnificent forests." Originating at New Smyrna in Volusia County, the rails went to Maytown, crossed over the St. Johns River via a drawbridge near Osceola, and headed to Chuluota in Orange County. The railroad eventually traveled south through Hopkins (now Deer Park) to Yeehaw east of present day Yeehaw Junction (six miles west of Blue Cypress), and then on to Fort Drum and Lake Okeechobee. Yeehaw was abandoned after World War II. Other towns along the railroad spur included Nittaw, Illahaw, Kenansville, Lokosee (Seminole for bear), and Holopaw. All had Indian names except Kenansville, which was named after Mary Lily Kenan, third wife of Henry Flagler.[25] Most of these railroad fuel and water stops later disappeared when the railroad took up its tracks after logging the cypress trees. Rumor has it that a couple of locomotives are still out there in the swamp (Ed Vosatka, personal communcation, Sept. 22, 2003). Today, Yeehaw Junction, located near the original Yeehaw at the intersections of State Road 60, US 441, and the Florida Turnpike, is not really a town but a crossroads containing a few hundred residents who work in the motels, gas stations, truck stops, and souvenir shops. "For excitement, they go down to the gas station and watch the grease rack go up and down."[79]

"Yeehaw" is a Seminole word meaning "wolf."[76] Towards the end of the 1800s, when the great cypress and pine trees were beginning to be cut, the last Florida wolf was exterminated.[60] The origin of the name of Yeehaw Junction, also fondly called "Jackass Junction" is joked about by locals for the mules that resided behind the local historic Desert Inn restaurant.[17, 79] Contrary to the Indian origin of Yeehaw, Beverly Zicheck, a manager of the Desert Inn, was quoted saying, "Yeehaw got its name because they did not want to put Jackass Crossing on the map. And what's the noise a donkey makes? Yeehaw? Right!"[17] The eight upstairs bedrooms of the inn were sleeping quarters for Seminole Indians coming from their swamp-camp at Fort Drum, cat fishers from Lake Okeechobee, and "cow hunters" from the surrounding area. It was rumored to have been a house of ill repute where ox-team drivers and later truck and Model-T drivers stopped for a swig of moonshine.[17] A still might have been located about 300 yards from shore on the north end of Blue Cypress Lake near a small bay called Moonshine Bay (Figure 3). The still operated for the benefit of the loggers and other thirsty "business" men in the area.[25] Any moonshine not drunk by the loggers was transported across the lake to a trail leading to the railroad, where it was transported north to Orlando or south to Okeechobee or Fort Drum.

Cutting Ancient Cypress

Logging the ancient cypress trees, hundreds of years old, was an important business in Florida that began before the turn of the last century. The durable wood was used for railroad ties and hotels along the railroad. Cypress wood is somewhat resistant to insect infestation, making it an ideal building material for Florida homes that are subject to termites year-round. Ancient Egyptians used it to produce the pharaoh's caskets, and during the Middle Ages, carpenters carved enormous cathedral doors.

On April 16, 1915, Fellsmere Farms sold approximately 1,146 acres of unsurveyed land, mostly swamp with huge cypress and pine trees on the west and southwest side of the lake, for $105,000 to the Osceola Cypress Company, a timber company from around Cedar Key, Florida. During the years 1916-1918, the company moved into this strategic St. Johns area and erected a self-sufficient mill town, called Osceola (Bridgend), to house 200 people. Its sawmill burned down in 1921 at a loss of $175,000. Later in 1924 and 1931 sawmills were built in Holopaw (Edward Vosatka, personal communication, Sept. 22, 2003). Aerial photos taken in 1943 show that extensive logging railway spurs ran for miles into the cypress swamps near Blue Cypress Lake. One spur is shown on the 1953 U. S. Geological Survey Map for Fort Drum NE, FLA, following along Blue Cypress Creek to the western shore of the lake.

The trees cut in the swamp were taken directly to the sawmill. Some were floated down Blue Cypress Lake near to the rail line. Bert Cayson lived nearby and remembered that he walked from the north end of the lake to the south end and never got off the floating cypress logs (Joe Middleton, personal communication, Sept. 22, 2003). What a sight that must have been. Some of the old logs have sunk to the bottom where they remain. The state or the expense has prevented loggers from removing these giants, surely well preserved, aging in their watery graves.

However, the fate of many of the giant trees standing in the water was different. Bert Cayson's nephew, Earl Cason (family name spelled differently) also grew up around Blue Cypress Lake. He remembers the trees dead in the water, still standing, but much taller than any of the surrounding living trees (personal communication, Sept. 26, 2003). The trees had been killed, probably in 1916 to 1918, by girdling (removing a band of bark completely around the tree which stops the flow of water and nutrients up into the tree). They were left standing until the early 1940s when a sawmill operated on the lake's western shore felled these remaining giants, cutting them into lumber. Some of the lumber was called "pecky cypress" which is wood with interesting grooves and small pockets that are caused by a natural fungus entering older living trees through wounds or fire damage. Many restaurants and homes used the attractive pecky cypress as paneling. Cason remembers a very large stump being trucked to Vero Beach's McKee Jungle Gardens, one of Florida's major tourist spots until Disneyworld came to Reedy Creek in Orlando. Fortunately, a part of McKee Jungle Gardens escaped development into condos and is preserved on U.S. 1 as beautiful McKee Botanical Gardens.

This type of logging was a form of above ground mining, taking all that could be taken and getting out without any thought of replanting for a sustainable product. These trees had cavities that provided nesting sites for the ivory-billed woodpeckers and roosting sites for the Carolina parakeets, both now extinct. Some huge cut stumps, "ghosts" of the old-growth cypress six to seven feet in diameter, still remain around the lake today, resisting the elements and decay and reminding us of their once great past. Even 20 years ago, the stumps had value as tabletops and people were coming in with chain saws to remove them. Fortunately Joe Middleton (personal communication, Sept. 22, 2003) was able to stop them by contacting and convincing authorities to consider the stumps as antiquities, an important part of Blue Cypress history.

The loggers only cut the best trees, leaving the "undesirables" around the lake, especially the hollow and double trunked. Today, these trees are the same interesting and sculptured ones that we admire and photograph and that provide habitat and homes for many plants and wildlife. Unfortunately, as song writer Okefenokee Joe sings, "All of man's technology cannot bring back those giant trees,"[51] nor the extinct species that depended upon them. "Giant trees can only come back if we treat them with reverence and respect for their value as living trees, rather than cut timber" (Paul Tritaik, current manager, Pelican Island Wildlife Refuge, America's first wildlife refuge, personal communication, July 14, 2003).

THE BIG RAIN

A month after the sale of some of the swamp to the lumber company in 1915, 39 inches of rain deluged the Blue Cypress area within a month (and most of that in a few days) in an area where 49 inches is the annual average. This was too much too soon for Fellsmere and Broadmoor. Thompson[102] quotes Gilbert E. Barkoski, one of Fellsmere's early cattlemen, as saying:

> "The rain started Saturday (July 31) when the water in the canals was two feet below the land level. By Sunday morning the canal banks, in the muck-land, had overflowed, and there was over two feet of water on the crops. Water was over the floors in the homes and buildings in Broadmoor. Some families gathered on the railroad bank with their possessions and livestock, and others were waiting on their porches, having stacked their personal effects and chickens up out of the water..."

After being rescued by boats and the railroad train, the people abandoned Broadmoor. Fellsmere streets were also flooded and waterlogged, and, for months, standing water remained in low-lying areas.[73] Herbert C. Wells (quoted by Thompson[102]) said,

> "The engineering firm of J.G. White and Co. understood the conditions. The original plan called for a dike around the Fellsmere property which would limit the ground to be drained to just the Farms Company development, but the financiers wouldn't stand the expense. They selected the $1 million plan in preference to the $2 million plan and lost."

Apparently, Indians living in the area had warned Fell's engineers that Blue Cypress Marsh was bigger than they thought.[73] A permanent dam was built to eliminate drainage from Blue Cypress into Fellsmere, but the damage was done, and from that day on, it was difficult to promote Fellsmere.[102] As Florida Institute of Technology's famous history professor, Gordon Patterson stated so well,

> "Prospective buyers who asked for directions to Fellsmere as they traveled down Dixie Highway were often told that they would know they were in Fellsmere 'when they were knee deep in water.'"[73]

Unfortunately for Fell and his associates, but fortunately for Blue Cypress Lake, they underestimated the challenge of turning a "great watery place" into rich farmland. Six years later, in 1917, after constructing 33 miles of levies, 67 miles of canals from the numerous creeks, and 215 miles of drainage ditches, the *Fellsmere Tribune* announced "the close of... the greatest and most complete drainage proposition in Florida."[74] After spending one million dollars, the company was forced into receivership in 1917. Nelson Fell and the directors lost their investment. Their dream of draining the headwaters of the St. Johns River had failed for numerous reasons: their plan was too extensive, they lacked the capital to protect the reclaimed lands, the land scandals of the Everglades had undermined public confidence in land sales, and the outbreak of World War I diverted potential European investors.[74] If Fellsmere had succeeded, as Fell had planned, Blue Cypress Lake might have become a vague memory passed on to us in "old timers" accounts of early life in Florida. But the source and headwater lake was spared yet again. In spite of the rain, though, Fellsmere became a progressive town with a $40,000 school building, six miles of sidewalks, and 1,300 books in the Marian Fell Library. It claimed the distinction in 1915 as Florida's first municipality to give women the right to vote, marking the beginning of the suffrage movement in Florida.[74]

FELLSMERE DRAINAGE DISTRICT

In 1918, following the rise and fall of Fell, a handful of Fellsmere farmers and businessmen led by Frank Heiser formed an informal sugar cane producers association.[73] Heiser assumed the leadership role in the reorganization of the Fellsmere Farms, now called the Fellsmere Company, and then organized the Fellsmere Drainage District (now Fellsmere Water Control District), which was responsible for keeping Fellsmere above water.[73] High water was a serious problem, because there were a number of unusually heavy rainfalls and/or the effects of hurricanes that hit Fellsmere in 1926, 1928, 1933, 1948, and 1956.[88]

MUCK RAKING

During the mid 1920s, Heiser and his business associates hoped to make a profit by selling the muck itself to the north as fertilizer instead of trying to grow crops off the muck. The muck was dug up and an "ammoniate" plant was set up west of Fellsmere to dry the muck before shipping by rail.[73] It failed because of high-energy costs, but it was another form of mining in Florida, "to take what you can and get out," this time by the bagful! Florida folksingers Frank and Ann Thomas, captured this in their song "There Goes the Neighborhood" with the line "We would sell our grandmother's shoes for the right price."[97]

How Sweet It Is

Under Heiser's leadership, sugar was finally successfully produced commercially in central Florida during the 1930s. Although Blue Cypress Lake had been considered an ideal location, Heiser established the state's first sugar refinery near Fellsmere instead in 1936. For over 35 years the refinery generated jobs for the community.[73] Even though the Fellsmere Sugar Producers Association owned the land east of Blue Cypress Lake, they seemed only interested in sugar, and fortunately did not develop the lake. During the 1950s, the Central and Southern Florida Flood Control District acquired the land around the east side of the lake from the Fellsmere Development Corporation, a subsidiary of the Fellsmere Sugar Producers Association. This side of Blue Cypress Lake became somewhat safe from further development.

Sweets and delightful homemade desserts can still be found in Fellsmere at the Marsh Landing Restaurant, along with frog legs, gator tail, catfish, collard greens, and hushpuppies, all at a reasonable price. In 1995, Indian River County Commissioner Fran Adams purchased the Fellsmere Estates Building which was built in 1926. Located one block north of County Road 512, it had served as the land sales office for the Fellsmere Estates Corporation founded by Fell. The building became the headquarters for the Florida Crystal Sugar Company through the early 1960s and later had many other uses, among them serving as a municipal building housing the Fellsmere Police Department and meeting room of the City Council. In converting the building into a restaurant, Adams has retained much of the decor, including the wood windows and doorframes originally logged and cut from cypress from the Blue Cypress area. She is also the major organizer for the annual Fellsmere Frog Leg Festival, which is cited in the Guinness Book of Records for serving the most frog legs at one time—6,000 pounds!

The Public Enjoys the Lake

Development of the west side of Blue Cypress Lake did not occur until after State Road 60 was built in 1925 as a single-lane dirt road when Indian River County separated from St. Lucie County. Early history of the present Blue Cypress Village comes from Walter Eager's[22] interview of Earl Cason, former owner of an insurance agency in Vero Beach. The woods in the area around the lake were alive with gator, ducks, wild hogs, turkeys, and "so many deer that you could actually select the one you wanted for the table."[22] During the 1920s, people anticipated that a railroad would soon be built along the east side of the lake and a hotel at the south end. In 1888 Earl Cason's grandfather, Thomas W. Cason, had settled about a mile away from Blue Cypress Lake. Earl's father, Raymond Cason, a crane operator during the 1920s, was hired to dig the four canals on the west side of the lake in anticipation of a building boom. Cason had five boats that he rented for 50 cents a day for fishing. Blue Cypress was difficult to reach, but regular customers could travel to the lake, tent overnight, and start fishing the next day. During the 1930s, Harold Conrad owned a large airboat that transported 6 to 8 people from SR 60 to the lake.[25] Other more strenuous approaches from Fellsmere included rowing to the lake via the old Zig Zag Canal.[23]

In 1938, Bud Holman of Holman Groves Inc. purchased land around the southwest side of the lake from the Crosbys. Holman granted Indian River County public access to the lake in 1940 and a right-of-way to construct a canal leading to and from the lake. In 1943, the Osceola Cypress Company sold several lots to W. H. Surrency; this land is primarily a cattle ranch operated today by his descendants, the Pressleys. In 1947, Holman and his wife, Dora Belle, deeded 26.5 acres of property to Indian River County, in exchange for building a dike and a grade road that would prevent flood waters from the west and north from entering Holman's property. The dirt grade road from SR 60 to the lake through the (then) Surrency and Holman ranches was opened to the public around 1954[67] and is now a county park. In 1957, Indian River County Commissioners sent a resolution to the Central and Southern Florida Flood Control District requesting that Blue Cypress Lake be declared a public body of water.[104]

Blue Cypress Lake Lodge and the Holman Ranch

Bud Holman, manager of the Vero Beach Airport since 1929, is credited with bringing the Brooklyn Dodgers spring training camp to Vero Beach in 1949 to utilize the buildings of the former naval air station. The Dodgers honored Mr. Holman by naming their stadium for him in 1953.[80]

After purchasing land southwest of the lake, Holman, on Dec. 7, 1941, finished building a lodge of pecky cypress from 28 nearby cypress trees.[23] To protect it from flooding, the lodge was placed on top of an Ais midden, a mound of kitchen refuse, mainly composed of shells, bones, and broken pottery, that indicated long-term human habitation. In the lodge's dining room, harvested from one of the huge cypress trees surrounding the lake is a 16 ft. x 6 ft. highly polished cypress slab dining table that four men cannot budge. Guest registers of the lodge list the U.S. Army Air Force General Hap Arnold, Eastern Airlines President Eddie Rickenbacker, Brooklyn Dodgers owners Walter O'Malley and Branch Rickey, and the New York Yankee Joe DiMaggio with his wife, Marilyn Monroe.[23]

Bud Holman allowed the U.S. Navy to use his lodge for recreation and access to the lake. The Navy even built an emergency landing strip near the lodge and a canal to the lake (John Tippin as quoted in Eager).[26] During World War II, Navy pilots stationed at the Vero Beach airport used Blue Cypress Lake as a bombing range and target practice site. Still today, during periods of drought, one can find dummy bombs on the bottom of the lake. After the war, Holman's entire 655 acres of the ranch was diked to eliminate the influx of water.[23]

Middleton Fish Camp and a Free Park

Located on the county's park on the west side of Blue Cypress is a fish camp that was started about the same time as the Blue Cypress Village, and was operated successively by Harold Conrad, Don Fisher, Taylor MacIntyre, and now by Joe and Jeanne Middleton. The county leases free space for Middleton's bait and tackle shop in return for their maintaining the county's property.[67] The county park's facilities consist of toilets, showers, a couple of picnic tables, and small areas for separate primitive tent and RV camping. Over the years, people and their families return to the fish camp and county park to spend a few days, a holiday, or week enjoying a laid-back happy time camping and savoring the lake's beauty. There are no entrance fees and few restrictions.

Joe Middleton has spent many years looking after this lake. Born and raised in Missouri, Joe Middleton moved to Lake Okeechobee in 1958 as a commercial fisherman trapping catfish. He learned of opportunities for catfish at Blue Cypress Lake and obtained permission from the then Florida Game and Fish Commission and Indian River Gun and Rod Club to set traps there as well. "They are the best eating fish anyway you cook them" says Joe. He got to know Taylor MacIntyre who was then operating the fish camp, and arranged to buy the tackle shop business and 5 lots with 4 trailers, which he did on Aug. 1, 1961. After the sale he had only $11.20 in his pocket, but he went on to support his family and raise 5 children. He has organized fishing tournaments at Blue Cypress Lake for many years. He has also attended fishing tournaments around the state on many lakes, but he has "never seen one compare to Blue Cypress Lake with so much nature left." Until 1978, there was no telephone, and anglers had to reserve space by mail, which was collected in Vero Beach by Mr. Middleton, because there was no rural delivery to Blue Cypress.

Middleton also owns his own fishing lure company—the "Lil Joe." He makes his own artificial worms and sells more by mail than in the shop.[21] The most successful worm he made, he claims, was a mistake. "I was making a black worm with a firetail, but we made a wrong turn! The result was a deep violet that has a deep red glow in the light. It is the best seller we have and catches more fish."[20] As an angler and developer of lures, Middleton knows that the lures must appeal both to the fish and to the fisher!

Blue Cypress Lake is considered one of the best fishing spots in Florida, and people from all over the United States come to try their luck here, especially for largemouth bass. The largest recorded bass from the lake is 18 pounds.[20] In addition, one can find excellent fishing for black crappie (speckled perch), bluegills, shellcrackers or sunshine bass, and even catfish, mudfish (bowfin), and gar. Evidence of large catches is found in the photos of proud anglers on Middleton's bulletin board.

Over the past ten years, we have never felt the need to put a lure or shiner into the water, as the beauty of the lake has been enough for us. But once to gain the full experience of the lake, we went out with Joe Middleton's best guide, Richard Parker, to test our luck for the big bass on the lake. It was a chilly Sunday in January, coming off a cold spell, a fairly good time to catch the big ones before they bed down to lay their eggs in "nests." Parker has over 30 years' experience fishing and seemed to know all the hot spots in the lake. However, we did not have even a strike! We have caught more fish in our canoe without a pole than we did in Parker's big bass boat on that day with a 150 hp motor and 3 poles in the water. (Elsewhere, not at Blue Cypress, mullet and a couple of tarpon have jumped into our canoe quite unexpectedly.) As resident Robert Davis said, "Blue Cypress is slow to give up its bass." Richard Parker showed us the big fish swimming under the boat on his fish-finder screen, but that day the cows were lying down, which indicated to him that the fish were not feeding. Yet we noticed the ospreys had no trouble catching them!

Other than shooting the breeze with the locals, Joe Middleton or Richard Parker sitting out front of the tackle shop, the best place for up-to-date information on catching fish at Blue Cypress Lake and the surrounding area is the fishing column written by Walter Eager in the *Press Journal*. Since 1982, Walter has covered the biology of the fish, equipment and lures, and history of the area, and also some of Joe Middleton's fish stories. Eager wrote one story about two couples whose men fished everyday in the lake while the women fished from shore:

> "One day I (Joe) caught a 10-pound bass and on returning to the camp, saw lines from the water and realized the ladies were in the cabin. I put the bass on one of the hooks and called the ladies, telling them they had a fish on the line. The owner of the rig was so excited and happy about her 'record catch' that she had the fish mounted! I didn't have the nerve to tell her the truth. Incidentally both couples continued to come back year after year."[24]

GATORS GALOR

Along with the fish, there are big gators in the lake. Middleton says that since he came to Blue Cypress, he has seen all the animal populations decline except for deer and ospreys."The alligators were so plentiful then that when you shined your headlights down the canal so many eyes were glowing, it looked just like a Christmas tree!" Out in the center of the lake during migration, there were "acres and acres of ducks for gators to feed on" (Personal communication, December 31, 2002). Joe Middleton also remarked:

> "If I had been gator hunting illegally in those days, I would have used large shark hooks on a long rope. I would have baited the hook with a large chunk of wild hog or a chicken and tossed it into the swamp, or in a canal. I first would have tied the rope to a sturdy tree. With that sturdy equipment the gator would be hooked and secured when he swallowed the bait. I would have trapped maybe six gators per night–if I hunted gators."[27]

Gary Middleton, Joe's son who grew up at the fish camp, tells the following:

> "When I was about 10 years old, a game warden was sitting next to Dad in our house and he started talking about illegal gator hunting. He added that he could catch a gator hunter easily because he could smell a gator hide a mile away. I looked at Dad and he winked. The game warden did not realize that Dad had 15 gator hides—all salted down—in the next room."[27]

From the time of the dinosaurs, gators have changed very little. A million years later, gator bones have been found at Tucker Borrow Pit, about five miles from Blue Cypress. Still very common at Blue Cypress Lake, alligators have been a key species in Florida's wetland ecosystems. Alligators are at the top of the food chain and influence other species' abundance, but they also provide important habitat reservoirs (gator-made depressions or gator holes) as they bury themselves in the mud to cool off. During droughts, these holes are used as water sources and refuge by many other species of wildlife. In some of our photos, alligators appear to smile because they think they are masters of the swamp.

Today, the alligator's increased interaction with people may lead to its demise. When fed by humans alligators become less fearful of people. They are curious and swim with only their eyes and nostrils above the water up to where people are. Lonnie Gore of Fellsmere, a state-licensed alligator trapper, has been frequently called upon to nab these dangerous animals. Through 1985 at Blue Cypress, Gore's largest recorded alligator was 13.7 feet in length.[53] Gore estimated then that he could see about 50 gators on any given night at the lake. Gator hunting by state permit on Blue Cypress Lake began in the early 1990s and continues with permits to harvest around 58 gators annually. During recent gator hunts, the average length of the harvest in Blue Cypress was 9 feet.[4] Even during mating and nesting season, we have not felt threatened by the gators although they are ever present. They are curious, but we stay at a distance. They rapidly disappear if we paddle close.

BLUE CYPRESS VILLAGE: SMELLY FISH AND A CAN OF WORMS

In the late fifties to early sixties, Holman provided long-term 99-year leased lots to residents, some of whom were prominent local attorneys.[52] What began as a tent village gradually grew into a small trailer park for weekend anglers. As time went by, more trailers, mobile homes, cottages, and even a few houses became common. Then additions and septic tanks were added without permits from the county's building and health departments. Nine structures had become permanent residences, including a four-room motel.

Something began to "smell fishy" in 1976, when Indian River County Attorney George Collins warned that the development was "a can of worms." Roads "do not comply with subdivision regulations, nor does the size of the lots or layout of the property."[52] However, it was not until 1984, when Danny Purdue approached the county to force the Peace River Utility Company to connect his trailer, that Indian River County officials finally took public notice of the village. The company had refused an electrical connection because Purdue did not have a certificate of occupancy from the county, which was not given because the trailer did not meet the county's ordinances.[61] The issue was brought before the Indian River County Board of Commissioners in October of 1984, and there was considerable debate. County Administrator Mike Wright said, "You don't have a fishing camp. You have a subdivision. If this was on U.S. 1, we would take it to the county's code enforcement board."[52] Mike Galanis, the county's environmental health director, said none of the buildings were issued septic tank permits and probably couldn't get them anyway.[52] Robert Keating, county supervisor of planning, said, "We need to re-zone the whole area into a separate district and disallow many of the things going on now."[82] County Commissioner Pat Lyons said, "We have no alternative but to enforce the rule. We swore to uphold the laws."[52] Lyons further acknowledged, "We don't know where their water is coming from or where their discharge is going."[82] However, Commissioner Dick Bird said he saw no "reason for dragging out all the dirty laundry" and suggested enforcement of county rules from now on.[52] Commissioner Bill Wodtke quipped, "It's time to fish or cut bait!"[92] Vero Beach attorney and former Republican candidate for Florida governor, Chester Clem, who owned one of the residences, said there was an unwritten understanding that county officials would allow lake residents to act on their own: "It's a happy little community. It's a clean, nice place...the yards are mowed...It's not a rat hole."[52] County Attorney Gary Brandenburg advised the commissioners, "The county cannot pick and choose where or against whom the law should apply."[61] Commission Chair Doug Scurlock said, "I can't see us going out there with bulldozers and tearing down an old lady's building because some other commissioners allowed it," but also he did not see the commission looking the other way to code violations.[61]

In the end, county officials decided to "sit steady in the boat," get "their hooks into Blue Cypress Lake problems" and not require the folks in the village to tear down their structures, or even to cite homeowners for violations of the existing zoning code, as some probably would be "grandfathered in" anyway. However, they wanted to correct potential life- and health-threatening building and fire code violations. After studies by a number of county departments, including a $1,125 contract for a consultant to write a new zoning ordinance for the village, the county built a wastewater treatment facility, and the septic tanks were eliminated.[77] Today, there is a small village, the only inhabitants on the entire lake, with about 70 structures spaced around three canals that lead to the open water.

Another controversy has remained: whether to pave the five-mile dirt road from Route 60. Some residents feel it would increase property values and would help those who work in Vero Beach or travel into town frequently. Others vehemently oppose the paving believing it might mean an end to their fishing paradise by bringing sightseers and anglers, and eliminating wildlife and beauty.

PLUMBING PROBLEMS: CONSEQUENCES OF DRAINING SWAMPS
FLOODS, DROUGHTS, AND CHANGING THE SEDIMENTS

The Great Depression and World War II halted drainage and development around Blue Cypress Lake. After the war, the United States Army Corps of Engineers and private land owners began cutting canals through the low coastal land ridge, upon which much of Interstate 95 lies, diverting larger amounts of freshwater from the St. Johns River watershed to the Indian River Lagoon and the Atlantic Ocean.[39] In Indian River County, this was done by adding the C-54 Canal, which ran alongside the Fellsmere Canal, and then completely consumed and obliterated the Middle Fork of the St. Sebastian River. As more dikes, roads, and canals were constructed and larger pumping stations installed to meet private flood protection needs, many thousands of acres of nutrient-rich flood plains were opened for agricultural production. In 1972, 62 percent of the fertile wetlands south of Lake Washington in Brevard County were unavailable for floodwater storage or wildlife habitat (Figure 6). By 1984, nearly 80 percent of the entire upper St. Johns River basin (727,839 acres) was converted to citrus, pasture, or housing.[58] Fortunately, most of the marsh on the east, south, and most of the west sides of the lake were not affected by this encroachment and reclamation.

Drainage of the marsh and reduction in size of the flood plain reduced surface water storage capacity. During heavy rains, runoff caused water levels to rise higher than under former natural conditions when storage capacity was greater, thus causing flooding. During periods of low rainfall, with less water in storage, water levels dropped lower than under natural conditions. These extensive canals and ditches disrupted the normal flood and water retention functions of the wetlands, and as a result, floods and droughts became increasingly frequent, severe, and more costly.[39] Major floods occurred in the 1920s and 1940s, and droughts came in the 1960s, 1980s, 1990s, and most recently in 2001 and 2002. In 1947, flooding cost more than four million dollars in damages.[39]

Two scientists from the University of Florida, Mark Brenner and Claire Schelske,[9] conducted experiments to study the historical sedimentation and nutrient storage rates in Blue Cypress Lake and the surrounding marsh. Using an isotope of lead, they were able to date marsh deposits and calculate accumulation rates of nutrients and metals in wetland sediments. There were no strong differences among the sediments for organic matter (90 percent by weight), carbon (exceeding 50 percent), and nitrogen (3 percent). However, total phosphorus consistently displayed dramatically higher concentrations near the tops of the cores. This was attributed to increased phosphorus loading from the recent use of fertilizers. Phosphates from detergents, fertilizers, or natural sources can cause excessive algae to grow and then decay thus polluting the water. In the lake, the rate of phosphorus accumulation since the 1970s was 2.3 times higher than the rate recorded for 1920, and other cores in the nearby marsh closer to the farm lands were up to 17 times higher in the same time period. There were slight increases in bulk sediment accumulation through time. Fortunately, total phosphorus accumulations both in the lake and surrounding marsh were relatively lower than other aquatic ecosystems elsewhere in the state.[9] From 1900 to 1985, mercury concentrations in the marsh's sediments had likewise increased four to five times, results comparable to concentrations measured in the Everglades, Savannas Preserve State Park and Okefenokee Swamp. Atmospheric depositions may be responsible for the high mercury concentration found in the fish and the consequent warnings about eating certain fish.

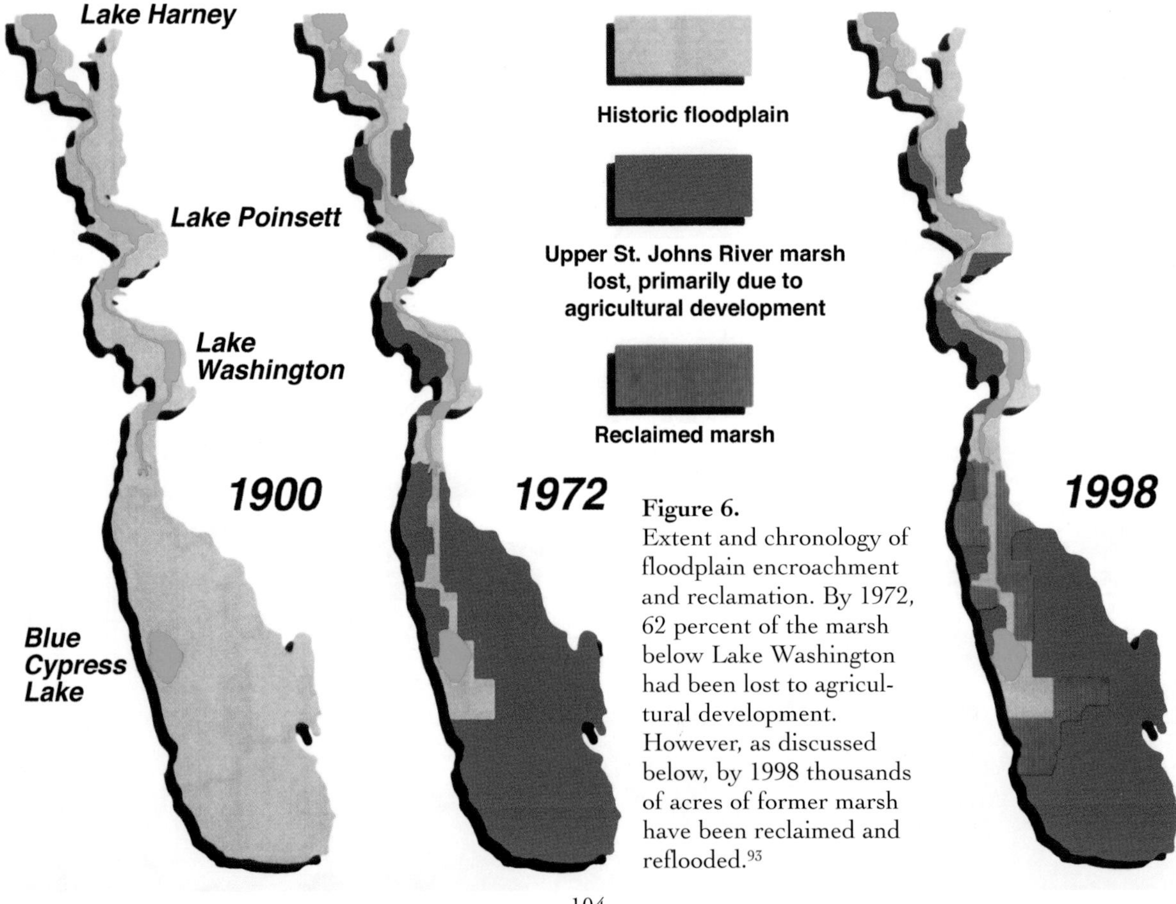

Figure 6.
Extent and chronology of floodplain encroachment and reclamation. By 1972, 62 percent of the marsh below Lake Washington had been lost to agricultural development. However, as discussed below, by 1998 thousands of acres of former marsh have been reclaimed and reflooded.[93]

Ecological Impact on Wildlife.

Installing irrigation ditches and draining swamps have also had significant ecological impacts on wildlife. Fish kills and plant community shifts have been observed recently and some of these are attributable to altered water levels and increased nutrients.[65] As agricultural development increased and the wetland area decreased, the St. Johns River Upper Basin's game fish, wading birds, and waterfowl populations decreased.[58] Using low-altitude aerial photographs, the Florida Game and Fresh Water Fish Commission reported in 1981 that the loss of wetland feeding areas significantly reduced the winter populations of ducks and coots in the Upper Basin from about 12,000 birds between 1948 and 1958 to about 3,000 between 1972 and 1980.[34] Similar reasons were given for the drastic declines in wading bird populations in other areas of Florida since the 1930s, despite the protection of their nesting sites.[56,57]

Wood storks once bred in large numbers on Blue Cypress Lake. Donald J. Nicholson reported in his March 1927 field notes seeing 125 active nests in the cypress trees around the lake.[43] Arthur H. Howell's book,[43] *Florida Bird Life*, a birder's classic, has an excellent photo taken by Nicholson of three young wood storks standing on their nests in a cypress tree in Blue Cypress Lake.

Nicholson lived in Orange County, Florida, all his life and in 1908, at the age of 16, traveled down the Kissimmee River in search of birds and their eggs, sometimes alone in a 22-foot rowboat. In addition to collecting in Blue Cypress and Fellsmere, he traveled around Florida, going south to Cape Sable to find nests of the rare Cape Sable seaside sparrow. His Florida bird egg collection was the most complete in the state, especially valuable because of his accompanying field data. He published over 80 articles from 1911 to 1964 on birds, most notably on the nesting habits of the Everglade kite, swallow-tailed kite, limpkin, Florida sandhill crane, crested caracara, black vulture, and black rail.

Listed as an endangered species in 1984, wood storks in the United States dropped from an estimated 60,000 nesting pairs in the 1930s to 4,000 to 5,000 today.[36] Regrettably, no wood storks were reported nesting around Blue Cypress Lake in 1984, and only 50 in the entire river basin.[58] We have not seen any wood stork nests in the last 12 years, perhaps because the ditching and diking drastically altered the habitat near the lake. In addition, limpkins must have been affected by the early drainage and irrigation projects. By the early 1900s, limpkins were nearly extinct due to hunting and loss of habitat for their prey, apple snails.[28]

Re-Plumbing by the St. Johns River Water Management District

Realizing that the system of canals and drainage actually worsened the danger of flooding and also caused disruption of the natural habitat, the St. Johns River Water Management District, established in 1972, has taken a different structural approach to flood control. Working with U.S. Army Corps of Engineers, the district designed what they considered a more environmentally acceptable flood control plan. Construction was initiated in 1988 and is now nearly completed. While the primary purpose of this "re-plumbing" is flood protection, its associated benefits include preserving and restoring freshwater marsh habitats, improving water quality, and decreasing storm water discharges into the Indian River Lagoon.[65,93]

Large tracts of agricultural lands were purchased to create four large Marsh Conservation Areas, two north and two south of the Fellsmere canal, totaling 50,000 acres of existing and restored marshes. These conservation areas were designed to function as shallow reservoir systems mimicking natural historic flow patterns and maintaining optimum soil and vegetation characteristics.[63] These broad areas, capable of retaining varying levels of water, will ensure flood protection. In addition, untreated agricultural drainage water is stored for reuse and cleaning in large reservoirs called Water Management Areas. These areas improve the quality of the water before it is allowed to enter Blue Cypress Lake and the St. Johns River system. The hope is that these natural communities can be self-sustaining and managed with only small structural modifications.[65] Canals that ran through the water management areas were plugged. Land that once grew radishes, for example, is now covered by a foot of water and is home to fish, birds, and insects.[75] The new lakes now called "Farm 13," "Stick Marsh," and "Lake Garcia" (also called "Miami Lakes") are becoming nationally known hotspots for great bass and black crappie fishing. In fact, many national outdoor magazines and Internet sites do not call it "fishing" but "catching!" Even ospreys seem to be heading over to these sites to get their food.

The district's plan reduces the freshwater releases into the brackish Indian River Lagoon via the C-54 Canal and St. Sebastian River. The C-54 Retention Area consisting of 3,870 acres is used to store water during flood events. This retention area, which was previously drained and used for agriculture northeast of the lake, is being leased to the Florida Fish and

Wildlife Conservation Commission for the development of an intensively managed waterfowl habitat called the T. M. Goodwin Waterfowl Management Area. Thus water management areas and reservoirs provide water for the surrounding marsh and agriculture when needed, help keep Blue Cypress Lake, the Indian River Lagoon, and the St. Sebastian River clean, and maintain flood-level controls and water quality. As a result of these efforts, Rodney Tillman, the Superintendent for the Fellsmere Water Control District, feels that "Fellsmere probably will not flood again."[75]

Prolonged Protection

Now that the Upper St. Johns Basin and Blue Cypress Lake are under the protection of the St. Johns River Water Management District, we hope they will remain largely undeveloped and in their current near-pristine state, for future generations to enjoy. Perhaps many of the nesting birds of the past will return. With adjacent standing water, plentiful fish, frogs, snakes and young alligators, and other favorable conditions, Blue Cypress may again become a wood stork breeding and nesting site. It is too early to assess the success of the Upper St. Johns River Basin Project, but according to Camille Sewell, Director of the Manatee Observation Education Center in Ft. Pierce, the numbers of great egrets, wood storks and great blue herons increased in 1998 and 2000.[86] The wading birds utilizing the Upper St. Johns River Basin preferred the headwaters as opposed to the northern areas, which may be less reliable sources of food. The number of snail kites and their nests initially increased in the Blue Cypress Water Management Areas from 1988 to 1992,[64] but then, for still unknown reasons, nesting success declined.[109] This may simply reflect the vagabond nature of kites or natural "boom or bust" cycles of snails and snail kite populations.

The beauty of the marsh surrounding the lake is impressive. We have traveled from the eastern edge of the basin to Blue Cypress Lake via an airboat and are in awe of the quality and quantity of plant and bird life. Sebastian River High School Teacher George Anderson, his students, and Dan Hayes from the St. Johns River Water Management District have created an excellent marked canoe trail, off limits to motor boats over ten horsepower. It is now open in the Ansin West section of the basin (west of Indian River County Road 512 near its intersection with State Road 60). The Ansin East section (east of Indian River County Road 512) has some unusually small, beautiful depressions (pits) covered with stunningly clear water and a population of snail kites.

Epilogue

A day canoeing on Blue Cypress is a journey in time and space, reminding us of our origins and suggesting our future. The challenges facing Blue Cypress and the rest of the state are great. Since 1936, Florida has lost 22 percent of its forest and 51 percent of its marsh, and has experienced a 60 percent increase in agriculture. But even this pales compared with the 632 percent increase in urban area.[78] Population growth, development, pollution, urban sprawl, and our own species' prodigal behavior are in striking contrast to the ancient cypress trees. The birds, the alligators, and, yes, even the mosquitoes testify to a rhythm that connects us to a web of life that binds all living things. So long as there is a place like Blue Cypress Lake, there remains hope for us.

We have attempted to bring the beauty we see in Blue Cypress to you. We all are fortunate that such a beautiful lake has been and continues to be preserved. This lake has remained unharmed because of the failed efforts to drain it and the surrounding area, its remote location, and the fact that its shores have been public land or in private agriculture. Some of the surrounding lands are still open to the danger of development and human impact. However, the recent restoration of the Upper St. Johns River Basin by the St. Johns River Water Management District and the Corps of Engineers, and, at the same time, the protection of the Indian River Lagoon from unacceptable freshwater discharges may be "one of the best public water deals of this decade."[93] It serves as a model for future efforts, especially in light of the high price for the Kissimmee River restoration and the cleanup of the Florida Everglades, both of which have had extensive ditching and diking and are under extreme environmental stress.

The Everglades were destroyed and now we have a $7.8 billion bill. The 2003 Everglades Restoration Plan[29] intends to increase water storage capacity, improve water quality and improve habitat, some of what the district has achieved for the Blue Cypress Marsh. Natural wetlands accomplish all three of these goals for free. If we understand this expensive lesson, we will understand the value of Blue Cypress and protect it. The Upper St. Johns River Basin project to purchase environmentally sensitive and agricultural lands accomplishes these goals plus provides opportunities for public recreation.

Our invitation to come look at the diversity and wonders of this area through our photographs and poems is also a request to reflect on what will become of Blue Cypress. How might this and other areas like it be preserved for all our enjoyment and protection? The future of Blue Cypress holds both promise and peril. Many of Florida's lakes, such as Okeechobee and Apopka, are managed primarily as reservoirs to benefit domestic consumption, agriculture, industry, and a huge human population at the expense of plants and animals and a functioning ecosystem. Groundwater levels have dropped 25 feet in some places near Orlando. On the east coast of Florida, Titusville (only 60 miles from Blue Cypress Lake) has "notified the St. Johns River Water Management District that by 2010 it will not have enough water to meet the needs of projected growth."[78]

Only 3 percent of the Earth's water is fresh, and only 1 percent is actually available, because 2 percent is tied up in glaciers and ice. Thus Blue Cypress Lake and its marsh are an important part of the 1 percent available to the burgeoning population in Florida. In a thirsty world, will we have enough sense and willpower to provide water for a few critical weeks or months late in the dry season for the snail kite, limpkin, and other animals that depend on it? Large agriculture holdings within the Upper St. Johns River Basin and a growing central Florida population put Blue Cypress at future risk of becoming just another reservoir for domestic and agricultural consumption, and not a healthy, living, natural lake and ecosystem.

If Blue Cypress Lake's level is lowered for long periods of time causing the loss of peat on the eastern shore, the lake as we know it could disappear. On the other hand, raising water levels to control water, extending the flooding period, and adding more organic material from surrounding agricultural areas would degrade and transform the lake into an eutrophic sink.[105] Increased turbidity and organic sediments that lead to low dissolved oxygen concentrations and overall poor habitat conditions would produce an undesirable change in the species composition and numbers of the bio-community. An eutrophic Blue Cypress would destroy the sport fishing of the lake, because the mayflies and other valuable invertebrates which fish depend upon as a food source would be eliminated. While the lake is one of Florida's healthiest, organic sediments have accumulated in Blue Cypress Lake at an increasing rate since 1935, mercury in sediments increased four to five times, and the phosphorus accumulation rate since 1970 is more than double the 1920 rate.[9]

The fates of the osprey and falcon, the bass and the alligator lie in our hands. If we care enough they may endure. If we don't act to prevent excessive development, pollution, undue water fluctuation, and invasive species, both Blue Cypress' and our species' survival will be in question. How might we live in harmony, close to nature by destroying less? Help us answer that question, and may you enjoy these reflections and appreciate similar natural treasures in your surroundings.

"The salvation of the Florida scene will come about only if the public savors its beauty, understands its limitations, and speaks up for it preservation"

Marjorie Harris Carr.[11]

REFERENCES

1. Baker, R.H. (1992). Malaria. *J. of the Florida Mosquito Control Association*. 63:39-47.
2. Bacon, E. (1975). *Orlando, A Centennial History*. Vol. II. Chuluota, FL: The Mickler House, Publishers
3. Belleville, B. (2000). *River of Lakes: A Journey on Florida's St. Johns River*. Athens, GA: University of Georgia Press.
4. Belleville, B. (2001, Nov-Dec). Blue, beautiful and mysterious. *Vero Beach Magazine* pp. 78-90.
5. Benesh, D. (1983, February 20). Body recovered from Blue Cypress. *Press Journal*. p. 2A.
6. Berry, E.W. (1917). The fossil plants from Vero, Florida. *9th Annual Report of the Florida State Geological Survey* pp.19-33.
7. Blanchard, C. (1990). Introducing the Study of Prehistory and the Discipline of Archaeology to the Public Schools. Paper presented at the Florida Anthropological Society, April 28, 1990. Naples, FL. Cited by Brown (1994).
8. Brenner, M., M.W. Binford, E.S. Deevey. (1990). Lakes. In R.L. Myers and J.J. Ewel (Eds.), *Ecosystems of Florida* (pp. 364-391). Gainesville, FL: University Presses of Florida.
9. Brenner, M., and C.L. Schelske. (1995). Historical sedimentation and nutrient storage rates in the Blue Cypress Marsh Conservation Area. *Special Publication SJ95-SP3*, Palatka, FL: St. Johns River Water Management District.
10. Brown, R.C. (1994). *Florida's First People*. Sarasota, FL: Pineapple Press, Inc.
11. Carr, M.H. (1990). Foreword. In R.L. Myers and J.J. Ewel, (Eds.) *Ecosystems of Florida* (p. xi-xiii). Gainesville, FL: University Presses of Florida.
12. Coastal Planning & Engineering, Inc. (1992). Hydrographic and Sediment Thickness Analysis of Lake Poinsett and Blue Cypress Lake within the Upper St. Johns River Basin. Palatka, FL: St. Johns River Water Management District.
13. Cooke, C.W. (1945). Geology of Florida. *Geological Bulletin* No. 29. Tallahassee, FL: Florida Geological Survey.
14. Crain, L.J., G.H. Hughes, and L.J. Snell. (1975). Water Resources of Indian River County, Florida. *Report of Investigations* No. 80. Bureau of Geology. Department of Natural Resources. Tallahassee, FL.
15. Darby, P.C., P.L. Valentine-Darby, R.E. Bennetts, J.D. Croop, H. F. Percival and W.M. Kitchens. (1997). Ecological studies of apple snails (*Pomacea paludosa*, Say). *Special Publication SJ98-SP6*. Palatka, FL: St. Johns River Water Management District.
16. Davidsson, R.I. (2001). *Indian River: A History of the Ais Indians in Spanish Florida*. Florida Heritage Series. Ais Indian Project Publication. robertid@pb.seflin.org, West Palm Beach, FL.
17. Davis, N. (1987, August 10). The Desert Inn, Yeehaw Junction's claim to fame. *Press Journal*, p. 1C.
18. Dickel, D.N. (1992). An Archaeological Survey of Indian River County, Florida. *Technical Report #55*. Archaeological and Historical Conservancy, Inc.
19. Dunbar, J. (1978). Florida Master Site File. Florida Department of State, Tallahassee, FL.
20. Eager, W. (1985, July 21). Middleton knows Blue Cypress Fishing. *Vero Beach Press Journal*, p. 5B.
21. Eager, W. (1987, October 25). Middleton's lures eye-catching to fish and fishermen alike. *Vero Beach Press Journal*, p. 2B.
22. Eager, W. (1990, April 22). Blue Cypress' beauty endures. *Vero Beach Press Journall*, p. 2B.
23. Eager, W. (1995, January 1). Discover Blue Cypress. *Press Journal*, p 2B.
24. Eager, W. (1997, July 6). Fish, beauty abound at Blue Cypress. *Press Journal*. p. 5B.
25. Eager, W. (1998, August 30). Plenty of history in those names that are so familiar. *Press Journal*, p. 10B.
26. Eager, W. (1999, November 11). Recalling west county's wild days. *Press Journal*, p. B9.
27. Eager, W. (2001, September 23). Outdoor life tough at Blue Cypress Lake 40 years ago. *Press Journal*, p. B7.
28. Elphick, C., J.B. Dunning, Jr., D.A. Sibley. (2001). *The Sibley Guide to Bird Life & Behavior.* National Audubon Society. New York: Alfred A. Knopf.
29. Everglades Restoration Plan. (2003). The Comprehensive Everglades Restoration Plan (CERP). Retrieved March 9, 2003 from http://www.everglades plan.org/about/rest_plan.cfm
30. Fairbanks, G. R. (1871) as cited by (Rouse, 1951).
31. *Fellsmere Farmer*. (1912, February 21). Fellsmere Farms will be Famous. Vol. 1 no. 1. p. 1.
32. *Fellsmere Farmer*. (1913a, June 26). From Lake Wilmington to the Atlantic Ocean. Vol. 2 no. 10. p. 1.
33. *Fellsmere Farmer*. (1913b, October 30). Broadmoor Townsite Platted for Sale. Vol. 2 no. 19 p. 1.
34. Florida Game and Fresh Water Fish Commission. (1981). Cited by Lowe, et al. (1984)
35. Florida Fish and Wildlife Conservation Commission. (2000). Minimum Convex Polygon Home Range and Secondary Dispersal Route of FP62 01 July 1999-30 June 2000. Florida Panther Genetic Restoration and Management Annual Performance Report 1999-2000. Appendix II, figure 11. Retrieved February 15, 2002 from http://www.panther.state.fl.us/news/pdf/FP62 movement.pdf
36. *Florida Naturalist*. (2002, Spring). Wood Stork Nest Count Tops 1000 at Corkscrew. Audubon of Florida. p 7.
37. Gessner, D. (2001). *Return of the Osprey*. New York: Ballantine Publishing Group.
38. Gill, F.B., (1994). *Ornithology*. 2nd Ed. New York: W. H. Freeman and Company.
39. Goolsby, D.A. and B.F. McPherson. (1978). Limnology of Taylor Creek Impoundment with reference to other bodies in Upper St. Johns River Basin, Florida. *U.S.*

Geological Survey Water Resources Investigations 78-91. Tallahassee, FL: U.S. Geological Survey.
40. Gould, S.J. (1992). Magnolias from Moscow. *Natural History* 101:10-18.
41. Griffin, J.W. (1988). *The Archaeology of the Everglades National Park: A Synthesis*. National Park Service, Southeast Archaeological Center, Tallahassee, FL.
42. Harrison, G. (1978). *Mosquitoes, Malaria, and Man: A History of the Hostilities since 1880*. New York: E. Dutton.
43. Howell, A.H. (1932). *Florida Bird Life*. Florida Department of Game and Fresh Water Fish Commission in Cooperation with the Bureau of Biological Survey, U.S. Department of Agriculture, New York: Coward-McCann, Inc.
44. *Indian River Advocate*. (1895, June 14). Surveying a Big Swamp Near St. Sebastian. p. 1.
45. *Indian River Advocate*. (1896a, May 8). Cincinnatus Farms. p. 1.
46. *Indian River Advocate*. (1896b, May 15). Cincinnatus Farms. p. 1.
47. *Indian River Advocate*. (1896c, September 4). For County Surveyor. p. 1.
48. *Indian River Advocate*. (1896d, October 16). Cincinnatus Farms. p. 1.
49. *Indian River Advocate*. (1896e, October 23). Sebastian & Cincinnatus Farms Railroad. p. 1
50. Johnston, S.P. (2000). *A History of Indian River County, a Sense of Place*. Vero Beach, FL: Indian River County Historical Society.
51. Joe, O. (1993). How the wolves would howl. On *I Saw the Eagle Cry* [CD]. Cowhouse Island Record Co., P.O. Box 1402, Jesup, GA.
52. Jones, E. (1984, October 25). Fishing village violates building codes-officials. *Florida Today*. p. 1A.
53. Jones, E. (1985, August 22). Trapper nails 12-foot gator here. *Florida Today*. p. B2.
54. Kale, H.W., II and D.S. Maehr. (1990). *Florida Birds*. Sarasota, FL: Pineapple Press, Inc.
55. Krueger, A. (1979, March 2). 10,000-Year-Old skulls found by Fisherman. *The Palm Beach Post*. p. 1C
56. Kushlan, J.A. and D.A. White. (1977). Nesting wading bird populations in southern Florida. *Florida Sci.* 40:65-72.
57. Larson, R. (1995). *Swamp Song, A Natural History of Florida's Swamps*. Gainesville, FL: University Presses of Florida.
58. Lowe, E.F., J.E. Brooks, C.F. Fall, L.R. Gerry and G.B. Hall. (1984). U.S. EPA Clean Lakes Program, Phase I Diagnostic-Feasibility Study of the Upper St. Johns River Chain of Lakes. Volume I: Diagnostic Study. Palatka, FL: St. Johns River Water Management District.
59. Lyon, E. (1990). *The Enterprise of Florida*. Gainesville, FL: University Presses of Florida.
60. Matthiessen, P. (1984). *Indian Country*. New York: The Viking Press (Penguin Books).
61. McCloud, C. (1984, November 3). County gets hooks into Blue Cypress Lake problems. *Vero Beach Press Journal*. p. 1A.
62. Milanich, J.T. (1994). *Archaeology of Precolumbian Florida*. Gainesville, FL: University Presses of Florida.
63. Miller, S.J., M.A. Lee, E.F. Lowe, A.K. Borah. (1996). Environmental Water Management Plan for the Blue Cypress Water Management Area; Upper St. Johns River Basin project. Technical Memorandum No. 13. Palatka, FL: St. Johns River Water Management District.
64. Miller, S.J., A.K. Borah, M.A. Lee, E.F. Lowe, and D.V. Rao. (1996). Environmental Water Management plan for the Upper St. Johns River Basin project. Palatka, FL: St. Johns River Water Management District.
65.Miller, S. J., M.A. Lee, E.F. Lowe. (1998). Upper St. Johns River Basin project: Merging flood control with aquatic ecosystem. Transactions of the 63rd North American Wildlife and Natural Resource Conference. pp. 156-170.
66. Milne, L. and M. Milne. (1980). *The Audubon Society Field Guide to North American Insects and Spiders*, New York: Alfred A. Knopf.
67. Moczydlowski, T. (1989, January 8). County ponders paving Blue Cypress Lake road-fishing paradise in danger? *Press Journal*. p. 4A.
68. Mohan, G. (1990). St. Johns. In Del and Marty Marth (eds.), *The Rivers of Florida* (pp 45-49) Sarasota, FL: Pineapple Press.
69. Morgan, G.S. and R.W. Portell. (1996). The Tucker Borrow Pit: Paleontology and stratigraphy of a Plio-Pleistocene fossil site in Brevard County, Florida. *Florida Paleontology* 7:1-25.
70. Mossa, J. (1998). Surface Water. In E. A. Fernald and E. D. Purdum (Eds.), *Water Resources Atlas of Florida* (pp. 64-81). Institute of Science and Public Affairs, Florida State University.
71. Mu, J., J. Duan, K.D. Makova, D.A. Joy, C.Q. Huynh, O.H. Branch, W. Li, and X. Su. (2002). Chromosome-wide SNPs reveal an ancient origin for *Plasmodium falciparum*. *Nature* 418:323-326.
72. Nelson, G. (1994). *The Trees of Florida*. Sarasota, FL: Pineapple Press, Inc.
73. Patterson, G. (1997). Raising cane and refining sugar: Florida crystals and the fame of Fellsmere. *Florida Historical Quarterly*. Spring, pp. 408-428.
74. Patterson, G. (1997). Ditches and dreams: Nelson Fell and the rise of Fellsmere. *Florida Historical Quarterly*. Summer, pp 1-19.
75. Pearson, K. (1987, March 30). Farm Land Becomes Reservoir. *Press Journal*. p.6A.
76. Peithmann, I.M. (1957). *The Unconquered Seminole Indians*. St. Petersburg, FL: Great Outdoors.
77. *Press Journal*. (1984, November 8). New zoning code initiated for Blue Cypress Lake camp. p. 4A.
78. Purdum, E.D. (2002). *Florida Waters*. A Water Resources Manual from Florida's Water Management Districts.
79. Ravo, N. (1984, June 18). Laugh-and Yeehaw laughs, too. *Miami Herald*. p. 1C.

80. Richards, J.N. (1968). *Florida's Hibiscus City Vero Beach*. Brevard Graphics, Melbourne, Florida.
81. Rouse, I. (1951). A Survey of Indian River Archaeology, Florida. *Yale University Publications in Anthropology* No. 44. New Haven: Yale University Press.
82. *Sebastian Sun*. (1984, October 31), County commission eyes code violations at Blue Cypress Lake, p. 6A.
83. Selim, J. (2003, July). Land of the lost...and found. *Discover*. p. 11.
84. Sellards, E.H. (1916). Fossil Vertebrates from Florida: a new Miocene Fauna; New Pliocene species; the Pleistocene Fauna. *8th Annual Report*, pp.77-119. Tallahassee, FL: Florida Geological Survey.
85. Sellards, E.H. (1916). Human remains and associated fossils from the Pleistocene of Florida. *8th Annual Report*, pp.123-160. Tallahassee, FL: Florida Geological Survey.
86. Sewell, C.W. (2001). Survey of wading bird utilization of the Upper St. Johns River Basin 1998-2000. Final Report. *Special Publication SJ2001-SP6*, Palatka, FL: St. Johns River Water Management District.
87. Shufeldt, R.W. (1917). Fossil birds found at Vero, Florida. *9th Annual Report*, pp. 35-42. Tallahassee, FL: Florida Geological Survey.
88.Siewert, W.A. (1988). A History of the Fellsmere Drainage District (Now) Fellsmere Water Control District. Unpublished document kept at the Fellsmere Water Control District, Fellsmere, FL.
89. Simpson, G.G. (1929). The Extinct Land Mammals of Florida. *20th Annual Report*, pp. 229-280. Tallahassee, FL: Florida Geological Survey.
90. Spoehr, A. (1941). Camp, clan, and kin among the Cow Creek Seminole of Florida. Field Museum of Natural History, *Anthropological Series* 33:1-28.
91. Stanbridge, R. (1997). Indian River County Historian. Unpublished working document.
92. Stanley, D. (1984, October 25). County looks at fish camp growth. *Press Journal*, p. 1A.
93. Sterling M. and C.A. Padera. (1998). The Upper St. Johns River Basin project: The Environmental trans formation of a public flood control project. *Professional Paper SJ98-PP1*. Palatka, FL: St. Johns River Water Management District.
94. Stokes, D.W. and L.Q. Stokes. (1989). *A Guide to Bird Behavior*. Volume III. Boston: Little, Brown and Company.
95. Swanton, J.R. (1922). Early history of the Creek Indians and their neighbors. Bureau of American Ethnology, *Bulletin*, 73. Washington.
96. Teale, E.W. (1962). *The Strange Lives of Familiar Insects*. New York: Dodd, Mead & Company.
97. Thomas, F. and A. Thomas. (1992). There goes the neighborhood. On *There Goes the Neighborhood: Songs of Contact* [Cassette]. Olustree Records, Post Office Box 1271, Lake Wales, FL.
98. Thompson, W.C. (1961, March 30). "Pioneer Chit-Chat". *Vero Beach Press Journal*, p. 1A.
99. Thompson, W.C. (1980, June 29). Pioneer Chit-Chat. *Vero Beach Press Journal*, p. 20A.
100. Thompson, W.C. (1981, July 5). Early farming in Fellsmere. *Vero Beach Press Journal*, p. 23A.
101. Thompson, W.C. (1981, August 23) Decline of Fellsmere. *Vero Beach Press Journal*, p. 23A.
102. Thompson, W.C. (1981, August 30). High water in Fellsmere. *Vero Beach Press Journal*, p. 21A.
103. Union of Concerned Scientists. (2002). The Science of Stratospheric Ozone Depletion. Retrieved February 13, 2002 from http://www.ucsusa.org/environment/ozone.science.html
104. *Vero Beach Press Journal*. (1957 October 3). Blue Cypress Lake request made. p. 1A.
105. Warren, G.L., and D.A. Hohlt. (2002). Aquatic inverte brate communities of Blue Cypress Lake: Spatial and temporal dynamics in the context of environmental influences. *Special Publication SJ2002-SP8*. Palatka, FL: St. Johns River Water Management District.
106. Webb, S.D. (1990). Historical Biogeography. In R.L. Myers and J.J. Ewel (Eds.), *Ecosystems of Florida* (pp. 70-100). Gainesville, FL: University Presses of Florida.
107. Webb, S. D., J.T. Milanich, R. Alexon, J.S. Dunbar (1984). A *Bison antiquus* kill site, Wacissa River, Jefferson County, Florida. *American Antiquity* 49:384-392.
108. Weigel, R.D. (1962). Fossil Vertebrates of Vero, Florida. *Special Publication* 10:1-59. Tallahassee, FL: Florida Geological Survey.
109. Welch, Z.C. and W.M. Kitchens. (2001). Snail kite nesting activity in the Blue Cypress marshes during the 2000 and 2001 breeding season, 2001 Final Report. *Special Publication SJ2001-SP3*. Palatka, FL: St. Johns River Water Management District.
110. White, W.A. (1970). The geomorphology of the Florida peninsula. *Geological Bulletin* No. 51, Department of Natural Resources, Florida Bureau of Geology. Tallahassee, FL.
111. Wilson, E.O. (2002). *The Future of Life*. New York: Alfred A. Knopf.

Appendix I. Common Plants Found around Blue Cypress Lake and Marsh

Common Name	Scientific Name	Comments
Alligator flag	*Thalia Geniculata*	Large-leaved aquatic plant
Alligator weed	*Alternanthera philoxeroides*	Prohibited invasive pest plant
Bald cypress	*Taxodium distichum*	Dramatic deciduous tree
Boston fern	*Nephrolepis cordifolia*	Often grows epiphytically; popular parlor plant
Brazilian pepper	*Schinus terebinthifolius*	Prohibited invasive pest plant; Red berries
Buttonbush	*Cephalanthus occidentalis*	Sputnik-shaped fragrant white flowers
Camphorweed	*Pluchea sp.*	Weedy plant with pale rose to lavender flowers
Cabbage palm	*Sabal palmetto*	Florida state tree; also called sabal palm
Climbing aster	*Aster carolianLanus*	Lavender flowered clambering vine
Climbing hempvine	*Mikania scandens*	Sprawling vine; flowers attract butterflies
Corkwood*	*Leitneria floridana*	Known in area only from fossil records
Dahoon holly	*Ilex cassine*	Red fruited holly beloved by birds
Dog fennel	*Eupatorium sp.*	Annual; aromatic when crushed
Florida strangler fig	*Ficus aurea*	Often germinates in canopy of another tree
Gallberry	*Ilex glabra*	Low-growing, black fruited holly of dry places
Giant leather fern	*Acrostichum danaeifolium*	Florida's largest fern
Golden polypody	*Phlebodium aureum*	Epiphytic fern with a golden rhizome
Green wild pine	*Tillandsia utriculata*	Epiphyte with tall green flower spike
Hydrilla	*Hydrilla verticillata*	Invasive aquatic pest plant
Loblolly pine	*Pinus taeda*	Pine of upland, well-drained soils
Maidencane	*Panicum hemitomon*	Frequent grass; important wildlife food
Marsh mallow	*Kosteletzyka virginica*	Small pink flowers in fall
Moonvine	*Ipomea alba*	White-flowered, aggressive morning glory
Muscadine grape	*Vitis rotundifolia*	Fruits of some plants are tasty
Pennywort	*Hydrocotyle sp.*	Round-leaved plants also called dollarweed
Pickerelweed	*Pontederia cordata*	Blue-spiked aquatic
Poison ivy	*Toxicodendron radicans*	White-fruited vine; well-known skin irritant
Pond apple	*Annona glabra*	Fruits eaten by aboriginal people & wildlife
Primrose willow	*Ludwigia sp.*	Yellow flowered shrub of wet places
Red hibiscus	*Hibiscus coccineus*	Large crimson flowers in late summer/fall
Quill leaf wild pine	*Tillandsia setacea*	Epiphyte that looks like a tuft of grass
Red maple	*Acer rubrum*	Fabulous fall color; ranges to Canada
Red wild pine	*Tillandsia fasciculata*	Epiphyte with showy red flower spike
Redbay	*Persea borbonia*	Leaves offer bay-like aroma when crushed
Resurrection fern	*Pleopeltis polypodioides*	Appears to turn brown in dry conditions
Saltbush	*Baccharis halimifolia*	Female trees covered with silvery hairs in fall
Saw palmetto	*Serenoa repens*	Black berries are high-calorie wildlife food
Sawgrass	*Cladium jamaicense*	Primary saw-bladed grass of the Everglades
Sedges	*Carex sp.*	Important fodder for wild animals & fowl
Southern slash pine	*Pinus elliotti var. densa*	Dominant pine in south Florida
Spanish-moss	*Tillandsia usneoides*	Epiphte of the South
Spatterdocks	*Nuphar lutea*	Yellow flowered floating aquatic
Swamp bay	*Persea palustris*	Tree with leaves pubescent on underside
Swamp fern	*Blechnum serrulatum*	Spores in two parallel lines on leaf undersides
Swamp hibiscus	*Hibiscus grandiflorus*	Large pink to white flowers
Swamp lily	*Crinum americanum*	White flowered amaryllis relative of wet places
Swamp tupelo	*Nyssa sylvatica*	Large tree with swollen buttressed trunk
Sweet or swamp bay	*Magnolia virginiana*	Tree of moist places with small white flowers
Viburnum	*Viburnum nudum*	Clusters of white flowers, black fruits
Virginia willow	*Itea virginica*	Shrub with bottlebrush shaped white flowers
Water hickory	*Carya aquatica*	Large hickory tree of wet places
Water hyancinth	*Eichhornia crassipes*	Prohibited invasive pest plant
Water lettuce	*Pistia stratiotes*	Prohibited invasive pest plant
Wax myrtle	*Myrica cerifera*	Also known as southern bayberry
White Vine	*Sarcostemma clausum*	White-flowered milkweed vine

Appendix II. Birds of Blue Cypress Lake

*Interestingly now known only in Indian River County as a fossil but present in North Florida
Birds seen or heard from a canoe or driving from Route 60 to Blue Cypress Lake at the Middleton Fish Camp are included in this list of 75 species. A serious birder who can get into the brush or walk the fields around Blue Cypress Lake, or can use a scope to observe the ducks out in the middle of the lake could see many more species. Birds that are seasonal are seen less often in a year than those that are breeding and live there year round. Likely nesters at the lake have an asterisk.

Very Common (seen almost every visit)
Great blue heron*
Little blue heron*
Turkey vulture
Black vulture
Osprey*
Anhinga*
Great egret
White ibis*
Belted kingfisher
Fish crow
Tricolored heron
Red-shouldered hawk*
Red-bellied woodpecker*
Pileated woodpecker*
Boat-tailed grackle

Fairly common (seen 50-60% of the time)
Sandhill crane
Carolina wren*
Yellow-rumped warbler
Palm warbler*
Cattle egret
Green heron (Green-backed)*
Bald eagle*
Ring-billed gull
Barred owl*
Red-winged blackbird
Double-crested cormorant
American kestrel
Limpkin*

Common (seen 20-40% of the time)
Tree swallow
Gray catbird
Common yellowthroat
Snowy egret
Eastern phoebe
Blue-gray gnatcatcher
Woodstork
Mourning dove
American robin
Great crested flycatcher*
European starling
Parula warbler
Northern cardinal*
Black-crowned night-heron
Black-bellied whistling duck*
Northern mockingbird

Less common (seen less than 15% of the time)
Yellow-crowned night-heron*
Crested caracara
Common moorhen
American coot
Common grackle
Brown pelican
American bittern
Glossy ibis
Wood duck
Lesser scaup
Northern harrier
Sharp-shinned hawk
Snail kite
Peregrine falcon
Northern bobwhite
Purple gallinule
Killdeer
Spotted sandpiper
Downy woodpecker
Wild turkey
Blue jay
House wren
Ruby-crowned kinglet
Eastern bluebird
Loggerhead shrike
White-eyed vireo
Prothonotary warbler
Yellow warbler
Black and white warbler
Rufous-sided towhee
Eastern meadowlark

About the Authors

Richard H. Baker, Ph.D. As a mosquito biologist with a Ph.D. from the University of Illinois in zoology and a minor in botany, he has been involved in wetlands and water bodies for 40 years. He spent 13 years in Lahore, Pakistan, in part as Professor and Director of a University of Maryland Medical School research unit, and 16 years as Director and Professor at the Florida Medical Entomology Laboratory of the University of Florida, Vero Beach, FL. He has authored over 100 scientific papers related to mosquito genetics, biology, and control.

In 1991, he helped Indian River County and the St. Johns River Water Management District purchase 291 acres of pristine upland and wetlands along the Indian River Lagoon, which was threatened by condominium development. In 1998, he authored and co-edited a white paper on Florida's mosquito control initiated and sponsored by the Florida Coordinating Council on Mosquito Control, a State of Florida Legislative body. It presented a fair, accurate, and important assessment of the varied controversial issues involving mosquito control and developed recommendations for the reduction of chemical use and risk in the future in Florida.

As Professor Emeritus, he provides environmental education for students and adults and training of nature guides. He leads monthly workshops and canoe excursions on the Indian River Lagoon and is a member of Indian River County Environmental Control Hearing Board, and the Indian River Lagoon and Florida Envirothon Boards. He chairs the Indian River County Land Acquisition Advisory Committee, and currently serves as President of the Pelican Island Audubon Society.

Juanita N. Baker, Ph.D. As an Associate Professor of Psychology at Florida Institute of Technology, Melbourne, FL since 1984 she directs The Family Learning Program, a counseling program for sexually abused children 3-17 years, their nonoffending caregivers, siblings and their offenders. The program offers a needed community service and gives doctoral students in-depth experience working with families and community agencies. The treatment program also serves as a training ground for practical applications of her research and graduate courses in ethics, program evaluation, sexual abuse seminars, and child behavior disorders and psychotherapy.

Previously she taught high school art, and used various mediums. She has been a strong advocate for libraries, education, women and children, the environment, and people coming together to work for peace and change in the world.

Richard and Juanita have together spent 42 years in Illinois, Maryland, Pakistan, and Florida. They enjoy camping and canoeing in Florida and many other places in North America. They have traveled widely abroad, and have learned to appreciate the diversity, needs, and stresses of peoples around the world, as well as the exquisite beauty of every place they have visited. They have engaged in many artistic activities together, including designing their current home, pottery, batiking, and photography, as well as bird and nature watching.

We humans are funny

We really haven't gotten far away into the wilderness,
as we have brought with us some of the best of our civilization...
the sleek Kevlar canoe from Minnesota,
bent paddles from Maine,
the Tilley hat from Canada,
the cotton shirt from China,
leather Berkshires from Germany,
my sun protector long sleeved embroidered blouse from Pakistan,
my faded floppy purple hat from Malaya,
my eagle silver ring by a native American from New Mexico,
our wedding rings hand crafted in Illinois,
our binoculars, film, and camera from Japan,
multi-use pocketknife from Switzerland,
Tevas, life preservers, and pistachios from California,
sunscreen from Florida,
Rome apples from North Carolina,
cell phone and watch from Finland,
and granola bars from New Jersey.